DATA IS LIKE A PLATE OF HUMMUS

By Lior Barak

To my partner in life, Christina, for giving me almost a year's time to stay home with our daughter Noa and compose my thoughts into the crazy book you are about to read. Without her support, I would not have been able to finish it.

Thanks to Michael (Mitch) and Francesco (Franci), my crazy partners in machine learning, data, and theories, with whom I learned so much in such a short time!

Gerrit, Lorenzo (Lore), Bri: working with you was the birth mark for this book.

Thanks to Sarah Mayor, my editor, for not giving up and helping me bring this book to life.

And finally, thanks to the *Tale About Data* team. Every employee in this company was dedicated and driven to set us on a path to success, to test the theory, and drive learnings from every organization and team we met.

© Copyright 2020 by Lior Barak — All rights reserved.

This document is geared towards providing exact and reliable information regarding the topic and issue covered. The publication is sold with the idea that the publisher is not required to render accounting, officially permitted or otherwise qualified services. If advice is necessary, legal or professional, a practiced individual in the profession should be ordered.

From a Declaration of Principles which was accepted and approved equally by a Committee of the American Bar Association and a Committee of Publishers and Associations.

In no way is it legal to reproduce, duplicate, or transmit any part of this document in either electronic means or in printed format. Recording of this publication is strictly prohibited and any storage of this document is not allowed unless with written permission from the publisher. All rights reserved.

The information provided herein is stated to be truthful and consistent, in that any liability, in terms of inattention or otherwise, by any usage or abuse of any policies, processes, or directions contained within is the sole and utter responsibility of the recipient reader. Under no circumstances will any legal responsibility or blame be held against the publisher for any reparation, damages, or monetary loss due to the information herein, either directly or indirectly.

The information herein is offered for informational purposes solely and is universal as so. The presentation of the information is without a contract or any type of guarantee assurance.

The publisher and the author make no guarantees concerning the level of success you may experience by following the advice and strategies contained in this book, and you accept the risk that results will differ for each individual/organization.

Services providers are not allowed to collect users' data whatsoever, and the General Data Protection Regulation (GDPR) that entered into force on May 25th, 2018 set precise rules about the data collection and processing (e.g. types of data, purposes, legal grounds, storage duration, etc.). It raised challenges from a tracking perspective, notably in terms of what data we can collect, when we can collect it, and who should govern the user's data. Do not forget to stay compliant at all times!

Table of Contents

Intro 7
    Buzz words 9

The Hummus Plate. 10

Data-centric 12

Data Infrastructure. 16

User-Focused Approach 20
    Data controlling 22

Availability, Actionability, Reflect-ability 26
    Availability of data 26
        Running Data on a Timely Basis 26
        Data trust 27
        Accessible data 28
    Actionability of data 28
        Store it all in one place 29
        Funnel it 29
        Impact it 30
    Reflect-ability 31
        Understand decisions 31
        Focus 32
        ROI (Return on Investment) 33
        Performance Analysis 33

What is Expected from Data-Driven Team? 35

Data Structure 37

QA Your Data 42
    Data Sources — Raw Data 42
    Measures and Dimensions — Aggregated Data 44

What Data Should We Collect? 45

Defining the Data Source. 47

User Scoring. 49

Becoming More Data-Centric 54
   The Data Discovery Workshop (DDW). 55
      What should you prepare for the workshop? 56
      What are the rules?. 57
      Preparations Before the Session 58
      First session — Get to know your data. 59
      Break time. 62
      Second session — Design Your Data 62
      Break time. 67
      Third session — The Visualizations. 67
      Creating the reports. 72
      Conclude the workshop 73

Creating Tickets for Data Engineers 75
   Creating the Documentation 76
   Data Sources 77
   Definition. 78
   Tables outlay 78
      Mapping aggregated tables 79

No EXCEL 81

Analysis — The Right Way 83

Data Automation. 86

Team's Structure 92

Summing up. 96
   Cook more data!. 98

Intro

Becoming a book writer was never my dream. In 2015 I found a new job at Lovoo, there I met Bri, Lore and Gerrit, they were part of the performance team, and later become part of the family, I was part of the analytics team trying to enable them to consume data. By working with them I have discovered the challenges of working with data and the necessity of deciding simple. I then got myself engaged in more meetups, conferences, in some I talked in some I listened, but I learned a lot from the data challenge we all faced. We didn't simplify our decisions. Since 2017 I was working on this book, kept learning and adopted it to reflect what I think is a method of working with data. I hope you too will find it helpful.

Often, data teams don't understand their stakeholders and stakeholders don't understand the data they need to have. For years, I've tried to fix this communication issue between the two, discovering that it must be addressed with both structure and communication. Success is realized only when people understand their jobs and company's goals, leading to databases that reduce data noise, thus helping people focus on actions — without the avoidable distractions created by superfluous information.

Simply put: the more data we have, the higher the noise created by it. Today, we can track *everything*, but excessive unnecessary data blurs strategy, becoming a source of chaos and confusion. It's like playing many songs at one time; there are too many discordant notes and different beats to understand the intended message — or enjoy it. In this book, I'll take you through the approach I've developed to reduce data noise, including these key functions:

- **It's not "just data; it's *data strategy*.** Know exactly what you need, why you need it, and how to use it in decision-making. Having a clear roadmap for analysis keeps you effective, focused, and ready to cope with whatever "storms" may come your way.

- **Own your data.** Keeping your leads private is paramount to successful businesses. You must avoid — as much as possible — giving away your customer information to third parties, as you never know what they do with it once it leaves your hands.

- **Become user focused.** Put the end-user in *your design*. What are his needs and expectations; what did he consent to? Remember: the tools you develop are used by your users alone, and they must feel secure in using your services.

- **Become data centric.** What can't be tracked, can't be evaluated. Don't get caught up chasing unavailable or unimportant data, and make sure you can store everything you do track!

- **QA your data.** The old concept of "garbage in, garbage out" applies here. Make sure people can trust the data so they feel secure enough to use the data daily.

While working with both large and small organizations through the years, I've met great people with the same issue in terms of data: bad communication leading to wasted time and useless information. A company can collect the most talented data engineers and businesspeople in the world, but without structure and strategy for the data they use daily, their collective work becomes ineffectual.

Data is a complicated topic in any organization, especially with recent privacy laws passing in California and Europe, adding layers of complication to the way we collect and use data. As many have said, data is gold. Still, many of us are drowning in a sea of data noise, finding it hard to understand which elements are essential — and which are not — leading to gut-feeling types of decisions.

Let's cut through the noise, culling both the data and the way we use it, making the most of our efforts and our time.

Buzz words

- Measures — These are standard numeric units we use for calculation, for example installs, visitors; we count a number.
- Dimensions — Forms or shapes we use to filter or aggregate our measures, for example country, gender.
- KPI — Key performance indicator this is a calculates measure mostly using one or more measures. By setting KPIs we know our goals, for example Total number of installs, or ROI.
- ROI — Return of investment, could be any way of the company to return their investment against the spending.
- One True Source — When you have more than one source for your data, the one true source is the data source you pick for the measure or dimension.
- Backlog — Raw unsorted tickets/tasks with information that requires being sorted and assigned into a purpose.
- Data collection — Collecting data from different sources, if internal, such as web site, app, software or third parties such as Facebook, Google, and others.
- Data centralization — The way we centralize all our data sources in one place.
- Big Query — BigQuery is a managed data warehouse on RESTful web service that enables scalability.
- AWS — Amazon Web Services is a subsidiary of Amazon that provides on-demand cloud computing platforms and APIs to individuals.

The Hummus Plate

Data is like a plate of hummus. While I realize this sounds ridiculous, bear with me! Hummus is a great dish by itself — and can even be a great meal — but it naturally goes well with other types of foods, becoming the foundation of superb dishes.

We can top our hummus with everything from plain to fried meat, or even a blend of nuts; its versatility is legendary. What may sound odd to one person may be a culinary delight to another, so just like data, our hummus can be designed to suit our needs and purposes.

I started cooking hummus when I moved from Israel to Germany, where I met and married my wife. Traveling less often to my homeland, I craved hummus and researched how to make it, finding hundreds of recipes from different chefs and home cooks. Each had something separating their hummus renditions from others, from the way they soaked the chickpeas to the way they cooked it, and even how they mashed and mixed it. It was the experience of learning different cooking styles (and letting my friends judge my skills) that brought about this book. I kept a small journal, tracking my cooking processes and recording which recipe worked best based on feedback. Interestingly, each recipe was enticing to some, and only elicited suggestions for improvement from others!

I learned that no matter how hard I tried to attain the perfect flavor of my home and childhood, people asked for changes, taking my method and ingredients in a different direction based on *how they believed hummus should taste.*

Hummus just like data; each person may have different opinions on its ingredients and how to mix it to hit their palate-pleasing target. There may be many suggestions offered for improvement, but the cook (or data specialist) can't always conform with others' ideas. Instead, he must consider his own "recipe's" foundation — one he may have worked on for years — remembering that his job is to lead others into his world, giving them a taste of his creation. Sometimes they will love it, sometimes they will leave it, but it is his job to lead the experience.

You may happily eat plain hummus, or you may add unusual toppings and spices like mushrooms, eggplant, smoked paprika, or curry paste. Such additions may change the creation, but you still consuming food based on the chef's original recipe. The hummus will accept all the variations, accompanying them in an amazing world of taste, color, and experience.

Data-centric

The best hummus restaurants I know serve only hummus, making the most of chickpeas. Each chef believes he/she has found the right chickpea, the optimal cooking time, and the perfect ingredients for their dishes. To arrive at this peak combination, they tried many recipes until they found the formula that delivered the exact result they sought. The same goes for becoming a data-centric team.

While data may be the new "gold" of every organization, people still struggle to become truly data driven, often overusing (but not understanding) the latest buzzwords: "data-centric." It's difficult for companies to be both data driven and data-centric where — largely — data is crashing, and decision-makers are causing chaos and uncertainty instead of clarity and focus. Again, you can hire the best data engineers, but that is no guarantee that your data will be clearer or better; perhaps their work may speed up your data collection and processing, but with no measurable effect on the way you make decisions.

"Data noise" describes the biggest issue facing companies today. We are surrounded by *so much data* that we can't focus or find the strings of data directly affecting daily decision-making, giving too much or too little weight in terms of effective outcomes. If your business is relying on the fact you can track and communicate with your users, we can agree that a user signup provides more insight and a greater effect on marketing, giving the right indicator to identify if it's the right users or not- more so than a new user without a signup. Interestingly, about half of readers will consider that sentence as wrong, 25% will say it's right, and 25% will say it does not affect the funnel. It's easy to see how these three perspectives might lead to confusion in terms of goals.

Becoming a true data driven and data-centric team starts with changing how you think and speak, and by asking the right questions. What's essential in your user funnel? Can you define your KPIs, identifying the crucial data for decision-making and discarding data noise to help you check your data less often? Remember: what can't be tracked, can't be measured. What can't be measured, can't be evaluated. We need solid factors (data) for effective decision-making.

As someone who moved from the web world to the app world, the app domain was a new experience for me. I discovered that people must move fast — but _react_ even faster! As I said once in an interview, I am a speed boat, but I need to be a Ferrari. Too often, decisions were based on gut feelings — the worst basis from which to make important choices. Lele, Bri, Lore, and Gerrit were already at the job when I joined, and they on-boarded me quickly. Thanks to them, I gained a year's worth of knowledge in just six intense weeks, and their help helped inspire me to write this book. My early learning is based on the year we spent together working to build up a data infrastructure, setting the reporting system to present the right information for effective decision-making.

Gerrit was always there to remind me of the importance of fresh and effective data. If he didn't receive his data in the morning, I was welcomed to the office with a loud "WHERE IS MY DATA?" I introduced the team to Tableau — a powerful, secure, and flexible end-to-end analytics platform — and they became hooked on it. Every morning, they queried for performance data directly from the reporting I had built for them, rather than from ad publishers (such as Facebook, Google Ads, Twitter, Adjust, and others. Their dashboards were missing a lot of information — or contained wrong projections.

We moved away from using Excel, forming the "NO EXCEL" policy. Before Tableau, team members had downloaded reports relevant for themselves, done some Vlookups (often resulting in errors) and after two to three hours, worked on campaign optimization and budget optimization, deciding where the next euro should go.

Those old ways created drawn-out days because the methods took too long and produced undependable results. In other words, they couldn't effectively do the job they were being paid to do: optimize campaigns. The team was wasting about 40% of their days downloading, organizing, and checking data in an inefficient process vulnerable to mistakes and miscommunication. Even having weekly meetings — providing time for members to present their data — didn't help them become a true data driven performance team, as they all focused on their own domain and didn't form one combined overview.

Some will say that downloading CSV files from the ad publishers is "old-school." Today, many use APIs (a set of functions and procedures allowing the creation of applications that access the features or data of an operating system, application, or other service) to collect the data from different ad publishers. However, small (and new) companies need more time to create such tools, perhaps using external sources to collect this information for them. Still 59% of respondents said that data collection and centralization is their biggest challenge, and 46% struggle to gain actionable insight from their reports.

That companies have data downloaded, stored, and processed in the database does not necessarily mean that data consumers can consume the data and make the right decisions.

My definition for a data-centric team relies on a few key facts:

- ✓ Team members have the basic SQL skills and can run their own queries and find answers when needed (Enable Analysis Skills)

- ✓ A data warehouse (better, on top of a data lake) enables full access to the required data when needed (Data Availability)

- Decisions are based on data in 75% — 85% of cases; the rest are left to unstructured data (Data-driven Decisions)

- Decisions are reviewed weekly and monthly using data and evaluating plans to improve based on the performance (Focused Reporting)

- The team funnels are based on golden events (the most meaningful events,) allowing all the teams to have clear targets and goals that *can be measured* (Golden Event Optimization)

Most important, the data is available daily, when needed, and simplified for making decisions. Remember that "data-centric" does not mean "live data." It makes no sense to have live data for decision-making if those decisions can't be changed every 15 minutes! Even if it was possible, can humans react that quickly? Similarly, having data only once a week creates a delay in terms of effective policies. You will need to find the right balance for your data, based on the field you are in; I found that having daily data was enough for making good decisions.

Data centric should start with having the right infrastructure in place. It doesn't matter if you are a small or big organization, having the right thinking about the data storage will insure you can run the marathon.

Data Infrastructure

Data storage is important, as it defines *data availability*. Determinations you and the tech staff make about infrastructure has a huge impact on the future of your team development. However, don't blindly follow your BI (business intelligence) or engineering team; understand the issues you face, making decisions that accommodate your specific needs. Form a DATA STRATEGY. It's likely that if you are a data consumer, you will not need access to the entire data lake — an unsorted data storage structure containing an aggregate of unusable data to an unskilled user), but rather to a small warehouse with several pre-aggregated views customized for your needs.

You'll need to choose the right data storage console, which involves Buckets, Objects and Storage Classes, for storing and processing your data, and the actual data warehouse you'll be using. Understanding the basics of the stack will help you decide when choosing the best tools, and while there are thousands of different options, I'll cover the basic concepts and lessons I learned when dealing with data storage and data processing.

First, let's agree there is no true, one-size-fits-all answer for your business data. Some services or tools will be too expensive or unnecessary. When we design the stack, we must look at the costs of scaling; what are the costs when our activity climbs from hundreds of active users to millions? In the start-up world, this can happen in a few weeks or months, and an insufficient infrastructure can kill your growth in — literally — seconds! There are two approaches available for collecting and storing data:

DATA INFRASTRUCTURE 17

Data Lake — Amazon defines this as "a centralized repository that allows you to store all your structured and unstructured data at any scale." All the data flows from different sources/streams regardless of being structured or not, is captured in its original form, and is available to anyone with access. This mostly comprises raw data, allowing users to go to very low-level data. It is unorganized, requiring users to have strong experience with SQL and connecting different sources. *I would not recommend data lakes as a starting point for anyone.*

Data warehouse — Wikipedia defines this as "central repositories of integrated data from one or more disparate sources. They store current and historical data and are used for creating trending reports for senior management reporting such as annual and quarterly comparisons." It's a highly transformed and structured database containing only defined data by the user and organized into business-subject areas. For instance, if you work in the marketing department, you can gather data from certain parameters that concern marketing — not sales or accounting.

Both approaches have their own advantages. Data lakes provide more dynamic services, enabling faster processing and a higher amount of data stored; you can store any type of data, and when needed, all this data is available for running analysis quickly on raw-level data. On the other side, the warehouse is a great way to avoid errors because its data is processed and organized into a single schema *before* being placed in the warehouse, allowing users to retrieve solely what they need — as defined by pre-set parameters.

I recommend using both infrastructures, having a data lake for storage, and a small warehouse alongside for each of the teams' use. This strategy enables both storage for safety, while restricting data to each team needing it, reducing your processing costs and storage cost on unnecessary data, which reduces data noise and instances of error.

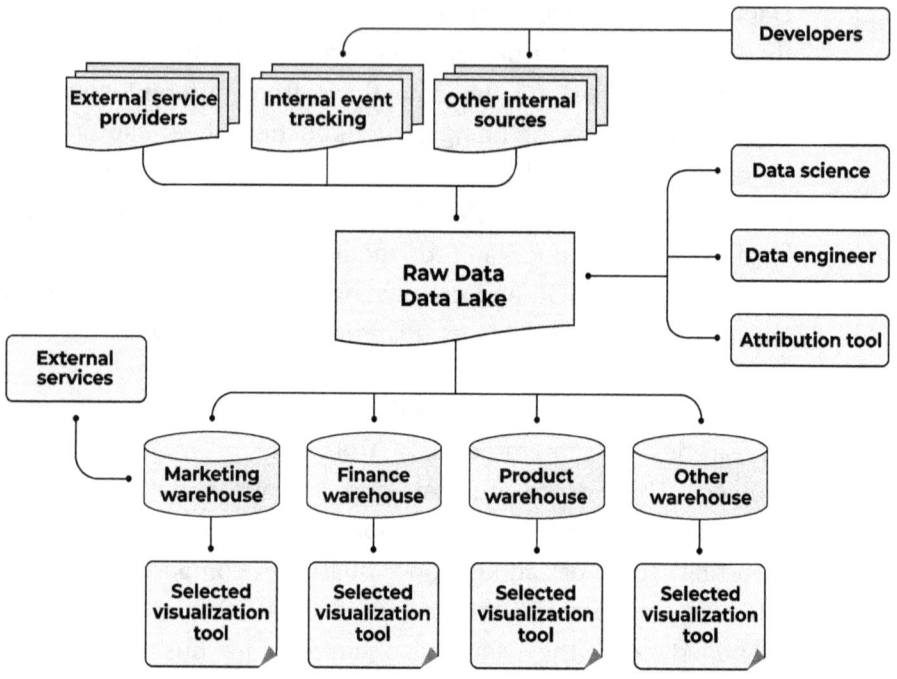

Data lakes are more useful for engineering teams needing unstructured raw data storage. For future cases (not yet defined, but possibly required later,) the availability provided by data lakes can save a lot of time in structuring and processing. For teams like finance, marketing, and product development, a dedicated warehouse is better to store and process data. Their use cases are clearer, focused on output of structured data, and they deal less with unsorted, unstructured data.

Consider standalone "team silos" where each entity can store and consume the team-specific data, without being throttled by an understaffed BI team trying to supply answers and data to a myriad of different stakeholders. Taking this approach will mean that the job of the central BI is to collect the data from external sources, hash the data to secure user anonymously, and then enable the team to consume this data.

The correct flow involves app developers, ad publishers, and attribution tools streaming their data into the data lake where it's being stored until required, then undergoing standardization before

DATA INFRASTRUCTURE

being transferred into the silo. This allows teams (like marketing) to access to the data based on a predefined data request, being careful to ensure they aren't exposed to sensitive information. Only then can this data be built into the required tables, becoming available for the team using the visualization tool of their choice.

For the data warehouse, they can choose from a variety of tools to structure the data; PostgreSQL or Hive are the more common ones. For consoles to manage and store the data, the two main options are Big Query (BQ) or AWS; however, also Force (by Salesforce) or IBM cloud can be a good fit. I always prefer AWS, as it provides better control of costs, which supersedes speed. However, if you don't need live data, this will not limit you from getting your data.

This leads to a discussion of visualization tools. It's my experience that most people will automatically defer to Excel, however, it's not the preferred option in terms of consuming or visualizing data — at least, not in the approach I am about to share with you.

It's important to allow each team the freedom to choose tools when consuming data, and while the company can propound Tableau, Power BI, Data Studio, etc., these can send employees running back to Excel. Each department should be able to use specific tools that suit their specific needs, and they will need to *develop their own reporting.*

My approach is to help non-data teams become independently data-centric, rather than depending upon a data engineering team (or the central BI) for supplied data. Relying on others' interpretation of needs can cause considerable delays and miscommunication; the job of central BI is to guide and enable the users to consume data and make their own decisions. Their job is not to enforce and govern the use of data inside the team *after* they have managed to explain why they need it and after getting the legal team's approval for it.

User-Focused Approach

My father took me to his favorite hummus place when I was a kid, and he explained that hummus had rules — you don't use a fork, you don't put meat on it, you need to finish your plate but leave a bit in the corners so the chef knows you liked it. I was flummoxed by all the rules, refusing to eat because I didn't understand *how* much to leave in *which part* of the plate to show the proper respect for the chef. If I leave too little or too much, will I be banned from the restaurant? The confusion left me too scared to go back for months! GDPR has things in common with the rules of hummus — especially the high fine you get for not following them; it can kill a business or your appetite for long time.

What does it mean to be user-focused? It's a very broad subject that can be part of many things. In this book, it refers to staying focused on user requirements, consents, and needs while overseeing his data in a respectful way. If we store the data in a secured database, we should hash his sensitive data, so it protects unauthorized eyes from accessing it.

The foundation for this approach relies on five principles of data privacy:

1. **The user's right for privacy** — We <u>must</u> respect the user's wishes in terms of his data. We should be clear with him about what we need, why we need it, what it will be used for; above all else, we must commit to not sharing his information without his consent.

2. **Share with care** — If we have the user's consent, ensure that his data is protected when we provide it to third parties who may have his un-hashed device ID; they should not be able to see his identification card or credit details, for example. When dealing internally, we provide only billing information for the finance team (but no other team should get it) and create rules for each team based upon only what they *need* to see for their specific purposes.

3. **Data has an expiration date** — Data cannot be stored forever, so we need to be clear about when data is deleted, and which data — like aggregated data — can be stored for longer periods of time. If stored for longer periods of time, we must clarify for the user what is being stored, what it is being used for, and how long it will be stored before deletion.

4. **Design with your user** — When considering new features, remember your user's right for privacy, designing those features to supply the highest security for his data. Communicate clearly, helping him understand how this new feature works and how it may be changing the way you use his data.

5. **Allow him to change his mind** — The user can decide — at any moment — to go into incognito mode, turning off tracking for a while or revoking the right to use his data for certain purposes. Also, it's always his choice whether to be tracked by certain features, and/or not by others.

While true that "data is king," remember that we don't always have the right to track our users' activity. Working closely with your user to help him feel safe with your services engenders trust. Staying transparent in terms of how his data being processed and the uses may help change his mind with your requests regarding opting-in for tracking and data storage. Setting high encryption rules over the communication to third parties will give him an extra layer of security that the chances his data will leak out is very small.

Above all, being user-centric requires that you consider users as partners; without them, you have no business and no services to offer! It's in the interest of both sides to improve the product, finding better ways to assess/meet his needs while exceeding his expectations of us as platform providers. That begins by listening to his needs and placing user privacy at the center of our data designs.

Data controlling

The world of service providers collecting any user data they wish is over; the European Parliament passed the GDPR bill, making it effective in the spring of 2018. While many may disagree with the law, we must still deal with it. The law is not counter forward for most organizations and raises challenges from a tracking perspective in terms of what data we can collect, when we can collect it, and who should govern the user's data.

This change in law forces service providers to 1) state what will they do with the data they process, 2) ask for user consent, 3) store the data in a way so the user can easily access the data stored about them, and 4) stop use marketing upon his request. This presents new hurdles regarding the way we improve our app with UX data, the way we personalize our content and marketing for the user, and the way we communicate with third party providers.

It's apparent that another bill will soon pass in terms of e-privacy law; teams will not be able to track a mobile user's unique device ID without first obtaining clear consent from the user *for each case*.

The California Consumer Privacy Act (effective July 2018) follows GDPR closely, and similar laws may be rolled out in other American states soon. This means that companies with operations in the US and Europe will need to maintain two databases hosted on two server farms: one for California-based users (if you have over 50K users) and another for European-based users. This will surely increase the difficulties of collecting, processing, and storing data — as well as increasing costs.

Marketing, product, and UX functions are facing increased risks of not having the data they need to operate effectively and efficiently. We need to be more creative in the way we process data and how we explain those directives to the user, all while becoming more restrictive on data shared across organizations and third parties. Becoming a data-law compliant team will require a lot of legal expertise and close auditing. Failing to close loopholes, secure data, and follow regulations will result in marketing departments with less (or little) data to work with and limiting both advertising and audiences.

Organizations employing paid user acquisition understand that it's not enough to entice a user to look at your product; you must also monetize him, re-target, and keep him coming back to you for repeat purchases. The cost of new acquisitions is high, so it's important to maximize your customer's return on investment, tracking costs and revenues. Business is becoming more complex, and many user acquisition managers I talk to are spending over 60% of their days adjusting budgets and analyzing their data!

Also, processing data is becoming more of a legal issue rather than a technical one. Our data strategies should include input from legal consultants to ensure lawful compliance and, likewise, include PR/Communications teams to assure our users that their data is protected, as well as what we share, and why. Building trust with users is tantamount to successful delivery of effective solutions.

In today's world, failing to take swift action can lead to financial losses. We are expected to invest each euro/dollar carefully for the best possible return on that investment. Sometimes we are even willing to suffer some losses, hoping the long-term will improve; without having timely data (or the right data) to decide, companies can die quickly.

We may be approaching a data universe where we pay users to share their details with us, enabling us to market our products and services, and learn their online activities. This would create a huge challenge to new competitors wishing to penetrate a market and raise the level of competition. Without the necessary data, he must find payment alternatives and ways to convince his users to opt-in for tracking and marketing.

To make legal compliance simple, there are a few key components to consider:

1. You must have clear internal documentation of your data flow, to include what data you collect, where is it stored, its uses, how is it being processed, and how is it being shared (if shared with third party organizations.) This documentation must always be kept up to date; set automated weekly updates.

2. Be clear with your users what you are doing with their data and why they should share it with you. Do not manipulate them and do not track without their **consent**. Being honest and upfront with your users builds a strong relationship in which they will be amenable to your ideas and more likely to give you the data you need.

3. Don't share un-hashed data. Even if you receive user consent to share the information, remain in compliance, hashing his data before transferring it to any third-party service provider. Analytics services with SDKs on your platform will need to hash the data transferred from the device to their servers.

4. Remove identified details about your users. You should be able to completely anonymize your users in such a way you cannot match details *unless you receive the consent for it*. You will need to build a filter service between your platform and the data storage where data will be anonymized. Data consumers will need to receive only the data they need for making their job possible.

5. Accept the fact you will have ghost users. Don't feel bad about it! Try to convince your users to expose data, but if they won't — don't track them! You built a service hoping you could use the data, but if the users refuse to share, understand and respect those wishes. The share of ghost users will increase with the new regulations that default opt-out from tracking and marketing.

GDPR — combined with e-Privacy laws — will limit what you can share, but you can always attempt to persuade users to give consent, explaining why you need it. Regard your users as partners, respecting them and explaining that you won't bombard them with useless push notifications or newsletters, but that the data will be designed with their full permission and best interests at heart.

Availability, Actionability, Reflect-ability

It's both understandable — and important — that different teams will adapt different views about their data; however, I urge you to create a team data strategy. My goal is to guide you in terms of how the goals, the product, and the data is combined to form a data-centric team that drives results, being more focused and rational in the decision-making process, while leaving a place for creativity and out-of-the-box thinking.

Availability of data

Data availability is no small thing; many teams still struggle to collect and process their data, but the real challenge is trusting the data and maintaining good communication.

Running Data on a Timely Basis

Gerrit was always complaining when his data wasn't ready for him every morning. While I didn't love hearing his complaints, they taught me the importance of timing — and *optimizing it*. Usually the first person in the office each day, Gerrit used that quiet office time to review data performance, but the data wasn't always available due to delays in the processes or breakdown of components. He needed to consume information that just was not available.

The foremost challenge in many organizations is ensuring that processes run on time, enabling teams to consume the data when needed. Old legacies, complex structures, extended growth, and lack of resources results in slower processing and mismatched SLAs, like a smartphone: super-fast in the first few weeks/months, but increasingly slower and less reliable. Like smartphones, users lost trust and ended up replacing the resource. Technologies must be maintained and upgraded. Otherwise, *your Gerrit* will be screaming from the other side of the room, "Where is my DATA?"

Data trust

As a data-driven person, Bri was accustomed to doublechecking all the numbers in the reporting. Occasionally, she found an error in the data compared to her dashboard — something that killed trust in our process and raised more questions for us to answer. We simply didn't have an effective QA system in place. When users begin finding errors, they return to CSV files that they, themselves, have downloaded; it can be very hard to regain their trust! I've seen this firsthand, how an entire BI team lost relevance in the day-to-day business. Sure, they were working, producing reports, collecting data — *but they had no consumers for it.*

Developing simple QA processes will keep your team from that point-of-no-return where data consumers stop using your data and reporting. It's like being at a commerce site, trying to add an item you want to your cart, but due to bad code, the item never moves to your cart, you can't buy it! It's likely that you would never go back to that shop.

Creating a simple morning email containing details about the data run will increase trust in your users. As a bonus, that may help catch errors early enough in the process shows you are on top of data; team members need these reminders.

Accessible data

Lore, together with Alex (our graphic designer), always enjoyed researching the creative level of their campaigns, better understanding which worked, and which didn't, but they lacked skills in SQL. This created a hurdle for them in terms of using the data being supplied. Making sure they had access was not enough; they needed a visualization tool to see results and to build reports that helped them reach their campaign goals.

Again, you can collect all the data in the world, but if your data consumers can't access it — and understand it — they will never find new ways to improve their campaigns.

Many organizations mistakenly build layers upon layers of data security, blocking data consumers from accessing certain areas or limiting the data they are exposed to. While we can understand the need for security, data consumers still need access to *any data required for them to do their job better*.

Train data consumers how to access and consume the data provided; otherwise, it's like asking someone to drive you to a destination but failing to provide them with the car's keys!

Actionability of data

Actionable data drives results. We shouldn't just look at the data because it's there; it must drive us to do something. However, looking at too much data — too many KPIS and sets — creates complexity in decision-making. This is not the goal!

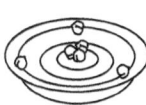

I once went with Gerrit to a hummus restaurant, and while I planned on having my usual hummus plate, Gerrit faced choices of no less than four varieties of hummus and ten types of toppings. He ended up requesting my choice; to him, the menu was unclear, leaving him confused by all the choices. He simply couldn't pick!

Store it all in one place

Gerrit always had an issue in terms of expense and revenue data, as some affiliates didn't submit the data on time, or the details were not at the right level — the rawest format — that he expected. Because of this, Gerrit was forced to work with some data from the warehouse and download the rest of it from the CSV files supplied by his affiliate. You can imagine the delays this caused in his decision-making, and this underscores the importance of storing all the data in one place.

If you're in an e-commerce business, you need performance and revenue information on a timely and consistent basis. All data — even the sort that is reported manually — should be stored in one universal database. Thoughtfully create a process that ensures that APIs are running smoothly and collecting daily data from ad publishers and attribution tools, and that your data consumers aren't forced to use external resources, as this both slows their work and opens the data up to errors.

Funnel it

Gerrit developed a funnel that defined good or bad user behavior; he wanted to see if the users landing on our app were the *right users*. Did they follow the funnel, or navigate to the wrong place? Were these authentic users with an authentic need for our product? Was the funnel at fault? Was marketing wrong, or did the product fail?

When the right users are not being reached, marketing people tend to blame the product, and product developers tend to blame the marketing, a horrible cycle without end; fireworks on new year eve in Berlin are nothing compare to the wars I have witnessed!. Having a fixed funnel helped Gerrit and the rest of the team take effective action, driven by data.

Using a clear funnel path for users to follow allows us to identify them as good or bad, helping product developers use data to create better products, helping marketing teams attract the right users, and decreasing negativity by building better synchronization between the teams.

Impact it

Bri trusted the data to make her decisions, defining golden events or cornerstone events — both important when deciding. If certain events happened, it meant her campaign was on the right track and successful; otherwise, her campaign needed improvement or should be ended.

It's vital to understand that some events have an impact higher than others. Although subscription, e-commerce, and gaming companies have different goals, at the end of the day, some session events significantly drive profit. We need to discover which events are high-impact (setting them as our golden events) and which have little impact on our bottom line.

For example, having 3,000 campaigns running concurrently sounds great, but how do you define where to put your marketing dollars? How will you decide which campaign to stop, and which one should be shelved? Defining events and their impact helps us become more action-driven in terms of data, allowing us to place our efforts where they do the most for us.

Reflect-ability

The last part of being a data-centric team is the having the ability to reflect upon past data to design future strategy and evaluating the efforts and their effects on ROI (return on investment.) Careful contemplation leads to maximizing collected data — getting the most bang for your buck — to reveal better tracking and finding new opportunities for data use.

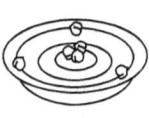

Once, I was sitting with Bri for dinner, eating hummus in some shady, shady place. We both agreed that the hummus was not as good as the kind we had in Israel, and we began talking about its blend, its taste, and what actually made it a good hummus compared to the dish we were having at that moment. We decided that it must be something in the water or the air in Israel that created such a different — and better — dish.

Understand decisions

Lore was testing a lot of his campaigns, trying to understand what happened within each one; he needed information to lead him to better decisions when things went wrong. It's vital to have a wireframe for testing each campaign against either some set of KPIs target — or even one clear and requisite result that can make the data research simple. Unfortunately, I've seen many campaigns (and organizations running them) fail to employ a wireframe for A/B testing, leading to information-less, irrational decisions. When marketing dollars are being invested into new campaigns, there must be data driven decisions supporting those financial outlays.

Others were basing their budgets solely based on the acquisition managers' ability to spend it all, without making solid, informed decisions in terms of funding one advertisement partner over another.

Focus

Like meditation, the more you practice on your focus, the clearer things become. You sleep better, decisions are easier, and you are more able to disconnect useless emotions from important conclusions. Whether we look at our campaigns daily or a weekly basis, we must stay focused. For Gerrit, I designed a dashboard (based on his defined funnel) that displayed simple traffic-light colors next to ad publishers' names; those visual cues provided him information that spotlighted trends and helped sharpen his focus.

While working with a German organization two years ago, I noted that decisions were all over the place; sometimes, a decision to optimize a campaign bid down changed during the campaign run; paid user acquisition bids needed to be increased to maintain a competitive edge. This company was missing significant structure in terms of decision-making, watching past performance instead of live performance, and employed multiple KPIs; *no more than three fixed KPIs should be used for decisions.* And it would have helped them to have a once-a-week reflection session to understand if moves have helped or harmed their processes.

That you have data coming in does not mean you can lose focus! Focus requires you to have a set of golden events on which to drive decisions. Weekly, investigate your KPIs. Monthly, evaluate performance.

The graphics team had a once-monthly session, going over all the creatives — deciphering between relevant and non-relevant ones — and working to improve the performance of the team. We didn't have those sessions on a daily or weekly basis because there wouldn't have been enough significant information to evaluate performance. Weekly meetings were reserved specifically for the performance team to evaluate the direction of their decisions during the previous week and — if necessary — adjust the budget and spending caps to align with progress.

ROI (Return on Investment)

At some point, Bri understood that she couldn't increase traffic without having something to measure it against. In the company, the main KPI was MAUs (monthly active users) and it was not enough, as she was driving paid traffic — most of which was fresh installs. How can you decide using MAU when you need to understand if you need to invest more or less? Drawing in users is easy; fetching *returning users* (who drive higher value) is harder. Back in the day, this was a serious issue.

While it's wise to have one KPI (or a "features success evaluator") for optimizing decisions, it must be clear and monetized. This is the easiest way to decide: either it's returning on your investment or not. If not, it needs to be fixed.

I don't believe in Installs, MAUs, or sessions. We should come to the office each morning, immediately able to evaluate the success or failure of our work: did we bring the right users or not? Did we drive the right actions, or not? Those answers should be there the moment we open our first report, because we are being paid to deliver results. Performance teams may on-board a lot of new users for the product, but to measure the effect of those new users, we must define the main goal of the product; are we just looking for registrations? Or solving puzzles? Or just hoping for product orders? Each consideration should be monetized so we can express the success of each in terms of ROI.

Performance Analysis

As a freelancer, I worked two months with a company in which the boss didn't know what he was doing — or WHY. Every day he would ask for a new type of analysis based on what he felt would explain his problems and failure. The result was horrible!

Each morning at 8:00 am sharp, he expected to receive a set of KPIs he defined, around 21 KPIs — *on 7 dimensions*. The system wasn't fully automated, so he demanded that everyone put in a lot of manual work beginning at 7:00 am., uploading data into the server and waiting for it to refresh. Then, it was up to his analyst to QA the data and share findings with him.

Aside from being stressful, this approach made no sense! Regardless of the information provided to him by the analyst, the boss always wanted to know why there were 2% less orders than yesterday. If you've gone through this, I understand; data wasn't meant to work this way.

Analysis — an investigation of an outcome trend seen in the report — should be conducted after a period where a trend is present, being structured to explain why analysis is necessary, how it should be conducted, its usefulness, and the expected outcome. More details about will be shared later in the book.

What is Expected from Data-Driven Team?

I meet many people in companies who deem themselves to be "data-driven", but teams were all *guessing* in terms of decisions. When I confronted them about the way they used the data to make choices, I found that, often, they were just overwhelmed by it.

In the mornings, the team would receive all the available data, having — on average — 15-50 KPIs (which were supposed to help simplify decision-making, but this was clearly not the case.) Their choices were being made based on what they thought was *the right KPI*, not *the right data*.

An optimal data-driven team receives data (ideally, early in the morning), including action points that reduce their need of reviewing tons of KPIs. This frees up their time to do deep dives, look for new opportunities, or spend some time in creative work. Having action points — like we have in the Data Discovery Workshop focuses on reducing data noise, limiting access up to three KPIs for decisions, and only 20 KPIs for research.

In data-centric teams, everyone in the team has access to data and everyone uses a personalized visualization tool, gaining immediate access to all information needed to make the best choices. Those choices must be driven by clear, fast, and easy formulas that reduce brainwork and the pain of making decisions. In this way, the data consumer can run experiments and drive deeper learnings about the process he is responsible for. Data-centric teams need not put out fires!

To drive actions, we need to enable the team to gather data and store it securely; even if some of the data isn't relevant today, it may be relevant in the future. We need to create "silos" (separate storage units/folders) focused on use cases; a perfect aggregation and correction logic, scalable infrastructure, and an easy, intuitive visualization tool that allows us to explore our data and make simple decisions. Wasting most of your day fighting to get your data in a format you can understand for decision-making — that's the making of a horror movie for anyone! This is why I suggest — as a consumer of the data — that you design your own dashboard. Why delegate that design job to someone else who may not understand what you need to see — or why.

I'll stress it again: "data-driven" means using data efficiently, having quality scoring for your activities, and measuring your efforts against a threshold (or goal) to assist in easy decision-making. For instance, if we know we need to have sales of 5,00 units to sustain our local team, then this becomes our target, and our efforts will be measured against that target. If we need to have a certain amount of MAUs to secure our budget, we know how many users we need to drive into our app to achieve the goal; then we have a clear golden event.

Data-centric teams focus on numbers and facts, avoiding gut-feeling decisions or guessing. In a study completed in 2017, it was found that 84% of CEOs don't trust their data, listing poor quality data as the biggest threat to their organization. 78% of the marketers listed their biggest job challenge as gaining actionable data due to a lack of trust in that data.

Sometimes, analysts are called "storytellers," as they paint a picture with numbers and data, but, candidly, I don't see a place for storytelling. Data should be consumed directly by the data consumers, avoiding third parties (to "fix" it), and you should have a support unit to question data limitations. As a data consumer, you should be the main owner of your data — AND the storyteller.

Data Structure

Simplified decision-making is the goal. The route to the goal is restructuring data into three layers, each layer propels its users towards that goal. Bri and Lore loved using raw data — something I needed to teach them to *stop* doing; when I talk about raw data, I mean all the information you collect from the different partners, in a very granular way. As a data consumer you should receive data logically constructed for decision-making and avoid working with different raw data sources to form your reporting. It's a tough thing to give up on your raw form data, but in time, it becomes as easy as breathing.

Collecting, processing, consuming data, and building databases specifically designed for funnels (which are specifically designed for simplified decision-making) is at the heart of efficient data-centric teams. Centralized BI teams: don't rely on them! Each team should collect their data from sources they are working with, making it available in the data lake as a centralized repository for the rest of the company. In this way, you can store all your structured and unstructured data at any scale, creating one true source of data — and at the same time enabling users to consume the data and process it whenever they need it.

You may tell me you don't possess the skills and expertise to build an API — and that's ok — you shouldn't, unless you wish to connect to your technical side. What you *can do* is hire junior Bis and train them in your team, giving them an option to grow after a year and move to the centralized BI, but you will be the one to give them the knowledge they need to become a good BI employee for your team.

They shouldn't build dashboards for you but, instead, enable you to consume and share your data across the company.

Another important facet of efficient data structure: each person should be able to build and consume his own reporting, with emphasis on what decisions he is driving when he walks through the office door. This is a huge change from how we are currently working with data! These days, upper management is often asking the BI to deliver reports, but keep changing the parameters, asking for more or different information, and overloading that department with requests for which the impact may be irrelevant.

By eliminating these two challenges of relying on analysis to build reporting and the BI to build our databases, we are solving several issues, but first — and most important — we have developed a single, reliable source for the data. Whatever is fed to the system will be used by everyone; no more irrelevant, useless numbers. The Finance department can report on marketing costs within the backdrop of what was booked, and if there's an issue, we can ask the Finance department about it — not an unrelated department. Second, we've avoided the bottleneck created by a BI team trying to serve everyone else's needs. Third, we are motivating teams to become more data-driven, providing access to germane data, motivating them to use skills and knowledge to build their own reporting, simplifying the way they make decisions in each level of the organization.

Establishing one true source for all data (the data lake) is a must when Finance, Marketing, Products, and Logistics departments are reporting on KPIs; they should be sharing the same numbers. Management reporting relies on the numbers from each team responsible for their own KPIs; who wants to be in a management meeting where every number is being questioned and no decisions can be made?

At the same time, we must be careful that data access — for each team — is properly restricted and carefully controlled. Bad habits and data noise are driven by **too much data.** Team members should be

DATA STRUCTURE

trained to understand data structure, and what can — and can't — be accomplished with it.

Back to layers: Building some structure in our data and tables should involve adapting three layers of data in the data warehouse so it brings focus to teams' decisions — and not bringing noise and clutter to that picture. And — again — team members must be trained on uses and limitations before using it. *(Also, each team should have a "data officer" who tracks the people who have access to the data.)*

When designing a new database, I like to think about it as a funnel: the deeper we go into it, the less information we are exposed to; not because we don't have the clearance, but, rather, because our focus is narrowing on the *specific decisions* that our work requires.

In past years, I have designed numerous databases, always keeping the least amount of needed information at the bottom of the funnel, while maintaining everyone's access to the rawest data. Let me explain.

Our first pillar is where we store all the **raw data;** it is unfiltered and unclean — we just save it in in case we will need to get back to it to check our data, or if our data needs will change in the future. (I usually call it the "graveyard", but it's your data lake, as it holds everything downloaded, including irrelevant data.) Make sure it is at the granular level, *the basest form of data*. For example, consider a database from Firebase; it will be the level of the device itself and the session — all the events fired — meaning, the lowest level possible.

I hope not many people will want to have access to this level of data, as it is difficult to understand without skills and knowledge of each source's limitations, and its issues. Most often, I'll see data engineers dealing at this level. In Europe, when considering personal data, the few who have access to it must sign a Draconic contract regarding data safety. This layer of data is the most important; if something goes wrong here, it opens a can of worms and can destroy *all of your data, putting you at risk with the data authority;* trust me, you don't want them visiting your business! Leave this layer to the data scientists and engineers, comparing and validating it, working on data reruns, and ensuring that the data is corrected after finding any errors.

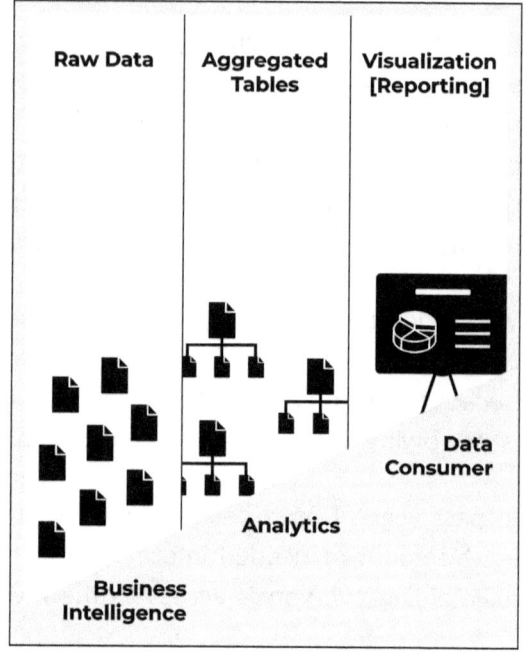

An organization has called me in the middle of my vacation, saying that, *out of the blue* they received a notification from the French data authority that they would be audited in the coming ten days; we were planning to start the process just the month after. An audit in ten days could have shut down that organization, creating bad PR that might have taken years to clean up. You'll want to avoid this scenario!

Our second layer is the **aggregated-corrected;** this is where we store more structured data after we have corrected it, cleaned it, and aggregated it. I recommend building a few tables that will populate the information, allowing anyone who wishes to analyze the data to do so, knowing exactly where to find things. My favorite structure for this purpose is a performance table, as provided by Facebook, Google and other partner data; a place where we store the campaign information such as campaign metadata, costs, impressions, clicks and everything coming out of the partners' APIs. I also suggest a second table for all the events created within the site or the app, as well as for revenues.

This layer (aggregated-corrected) is accessed by those wanting to research more about their data, perhaps for gaining a better

DATA STRUCTURE

understanding the user-journey. This is very useful in terms of support decisions, changing activity, or when redesigning the product.

The third layer (or pillar) is the consumer data. This layer is where we store our views or, stated differently, the decision-makers' reports. At this level, we have logically driven data to drive actionable decisions, no more than 3 KPIs, a limited number of dimensions — and all of it designed to ensure we have only the most important information for planning and making decisions. We have very narrow tables, focused on decisions and funnels to allow the consumer to make the right decision without thinking much. Well, one needs to think, but the helpful data is there, waiting for you to use it.

I enjoy connecting these tables to the visualization tools, creating a clear report to display important information the organization can use to make effective, informed choices.

Just like a hummus plate, we build *in layers*. We place the hummus as a foundation, we top it with our add-ons, and wrap it up with a nice amount of olive oil that emphasizes the taste.

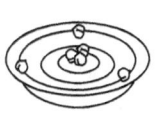

Once, I went into a restaurant in Amsterdam with a friend to eat hummus. The place was above a coffee shop and many people ate hummus under the influence of one thing or another. We were sitting at a corner table, and while I won't say that the hummus was good, but some people were describing the experience using wild metaphors!

Why am I telling you this? Sometimes, we hope the simple numbers (which are *not so good*) will be better than expected, and we paint an image of them that has no basis in reality. When dealing with numbers, we can visualize them nicely, but if something is wrong, *it's wrong*.

QA Your Data

Quality Assurance may be the most overlooked step of getting your data in place. Sadly, many data engineers believe that it's the job of the data consumers to QA their data, informing those engineers if something is wrong!

I wish to challenge this approach, offering an alternative where the balance of the QA is being split between all departments; data engineers should function as "data gatekeepers", NOT the stakeholders. The data provider should be the first one to notice that something is wrong, later notifying the data consumers of such information. Automatic tools for reviewing patterns makes flagging errors simpler.

The more data we have, the harder (and more complex) it becomes for data engineers to QA those datasets. Cleaning up and reducing data noise provides a more streamlined "place" from which these engineers work, leading to better outcomes and higher data consumer trust. Without that trust, engineering teams lose their value.

Data Sources — Raw Data

We are collecting a lot of data; automating a process check to ensure that collection went well is both simple and necessary to keep data consumers aware of any issues.

Was the API call working? Did we find a file in our S3 bucket? It's easy to test to see if a process failed or if a file was created and doing that immediately marks missing data at the consumer level. This informs the user — which allows them to prepare themselves and decide whether to move forward or wait for corrected data.

Some data sources are more important than others, but there is no need to stop the process because of a failed API call. Simply mark it in the logs and send a notification to the users, setting in advance which calls are more important and which are less important; this allows us to drive better and faster results by knowing when to start and when to stop data processing.

Size checking is very important, and often you can see — by size alone — that something has gone amiss with the process. I usually note the smallest, the largest, and the average file size for the last X days; if the new downloads aren't in the general vicinity in terms of size, I mark it as a possible issue. Perhaps there was just a change in traffic causing the discrepancy; to be on the safe side, I'll mark the data as "suspect".

Date — Did we cover all the days we wished to capture? Often, we have a successful run of our API call, just to discover we are missing the last day we wished to download! Always doublecheck the ending date for your data run.

Column name change. Too often, I've seen APIs or aggregations fail due to a simple change in the column name! This can be frustrating, but with so many "hands in the pot", even a small change — one letter — in a column name, and our entire process fails. Learn to check this simple factor early in your search for what went wrong — it could save hours, even days of research. We'll talk about this more in the Data Discovery Workshop.

Measures and Dimensions — Aggregated Data

Although we are collecting a lot of data, we need to check the measures and dimensions numbers to ensure consistency and spot issues. Even a small email to indicate that measures were checked and seem correct can change the way the stakeholders look at our data.

Change of in-dimension count. A few times, I've found that countries — *entire countries* — had just disappeared from the table! An easy solution is to know your dimensions; if you know there are ten countries in the dimension, find ten countries in the table. This simple principle applies to the OS, whether it is Android, Windows, or IOS: we know where our traffic coming from, so if one of them is missing, *we have an issue*.

Measure is NULL. Because these types of issues directly affect our stakeholders' daily decisions, it's important for us to spot these things quickly. This is easy to see, especially if you keep track of the last day's numbers compared with an average X day's number. And while a large change in numbers might mean something is wrong, a *complete null* means we *definitely* have an issue with the data quality.

What Data Should We Collect?

The million-dollar question — and everyone in our field is asking this. The simplest answer: collect it all but don't use it all; use just enough. Too much data creates data noise, and too much data noise creates distraction and confusion, which creates delay, which leads to trust issues, and so on.

Some organizations I've worked with are happy just knowing how much they've spent on acquiring each user and how many active users they have daily. Our thoughts about data need to be a bit different. Each partner we work with is getting paid to provide us with information, so we should be able to collect as much raw data within the widest net possible. Perhaps our attribution supplier needs to provide us with data on the level of a user and session, while Facebook and Google need to provide us with information about where our ad was shown, how many people saw it, how many people clicked — all this information is worth a lot of money, and helps make our job simpler.

I'm asked all the time: How should we collect? If, at the moment, we don't have the resources onboard to achieve it, what should we do? My answer is always the same: If you don't have the resources to do it now, make sure you have them in a few weeks/months. Until then, make sure you have a good service provider who can collect all the data for you, aggregate it, and give you full access to it in a later stage.

Collecting all this information in one place will help in the areas of creating automated processes for campaign setups and optimization, to approving and paying invoices automatically without wasting human resources to check payment requests or other manual bookkeeping processes — and even when you want to quickly discover if a user isn't following the right funnel. Even if you don't use it today, it may be useful in the future, and having all the information in one place will help you build more types of automation.

Most teams I work with are marketing or product-oriented, and they tend to be a bit inconsistent in what data they wish to consume. This requires a high level of ability and flexibility from the BI team in terms of making data available. It's crucial to give serious thought to making as much historic data available as possible; but only to the users who need it, *as they need it*.

I learned the value of historic data when we started working on customer lifetime value (CLV) forecasting. This wasn't AI. Instead, it was an ML model requiring at least one year of data points to estimate the CLV. During the project, we discovered we failed to track some important events for correctly estimating user value, which dropped our model accuracy to below 50%. It took us six months to recover from that blunder.

Lesson learned. This wake-up call demonstrated the value of storing data — even data you may not feel you need now. Storage is cheap. Missing important data is costly. There's no reason NOT to store all the available data from the different users on the server, allowing you to grab it later — should the need arise.

While downloading massive amounts of data may create small delays in the daily runs, we overcame this hurdle by downloading (during the week) only the required data for the day to day operation, and all data only at night or on the weekends. Sure, our servers worked harder, but no one was using them at those off times. This allowed us to maintain costs and server availability during the week, and whenever a model required data points we didn't have in place, we enabled the team to have the points they needed with minimum effort. We simply confirmed the need for the specific data, and then integrated the capture into our daily data processing.

Defining the Data Source

An oft-encountered challenge with many organizations is how to define "Measure and Dimensions." Are we talking about our install numbers from Google Play, iTunes store, or another source? How do we define an install?

Let me emphasize: You must have one true source. You cannot afford to have your team's spending reports based on ad partners, but the Finance team's reports based on the credit card charges. Any time two teams are using *different source numbers*, stakeholders will not know which report is correct.

Defining the source of your KPIs and aligning it with other teams will ensure you are reporting on the same number during meetings; if discrepancies occur, it's easier to share sources and discover where the error came from — *without* raising mistrust by the other teams using the data.

Another advantage of maintaining a single data source is using unbiased tools for reporting certain numbers. For example, if you are using an ad partner for advertisement, it's likely he has a higher interest in showing good results. This doesn't mean he is reporting fake numbers, but his agenda may interfere with providing the most accurate — and useful — results. If you suspect this is a possibility, use another tool to track conversions; consider internal resources for this.

In the Data Discovery Workshop, you'll be going over measures, dimension, and data sources, learning how to be validate (thus, trust) the data you are given. Align your thoughts now in terms of which tools supply you with which type of data — and which data sources you trust the most.

User Scoring

Organizations can't survive for long if they don't create a strategy for user retention. Since we can't use complicated forecasting models at the beginning, we'll start with something simpler: a ranking based on the funnel step we bring the user into.

Each visitor will receive a score based on an activity he/she did — and how relevant it was for our end goal of having this user return and use our app for a long time. We understand that in today's world, the goal isn't just bringing the user to our landing page; we need to convert him into an income, from simply listening to advertisements into buying a product.

Capturing user activity (data) is the key to measuring our success. We must be able to score our users, identifying whether they are following the funnel steps and arriving where we want them to arrive. Each step closer to the funnel's end means we are a step closer in turning our user from a prospect into a valuable customer. Each step increases our understanding of our product and the ability to convert the user.

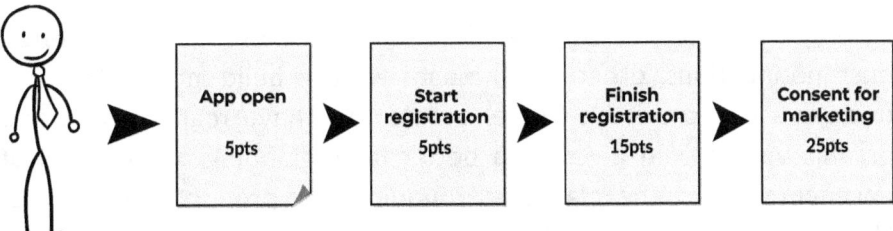

When we run an online campaign or we set a new product feature, we wish to see how users react and interact with it: Did we convince them to buy the product they saw in the ad? Using a scoring system will help us to put a "revenue number" next to our user that reflects — based on our investment — the Y value that the user represents.

This score should be used only internally (and in an aggregated view) to evaluate A/B testing, or simply for seeing the overall response of the user to our product. When the company grows and discusses financial models for profitability, the user score will be the basis from which to define the retargeting funnel and the potential of this client to convert into a paying user.

Broken down simply, we are scoring the user on simple operations like opening the app (5 points), marketing opt-in (25 points), remembering that marketing opt-in has a high value for us. With this, we can know our user better (which also means we will need to invest more money in communication with him, using newsletters, push or in-app notifications.

This work provides the basis for our investment decisions, and our end-goal is clear: we wish to turn a client into an income. We do this by retention, as well as gaining his consent for targeting by receiving marketing information. However, is it worth it for us to invest in retargeting the user if all he ever did was just install — then open — our app? If your business is fraud, then the answer is YES. If you're like me, you are hoping to engage with the user, building a long-term relationship.

Having data divided by organic, paid, and non-paid (newsletter, push notifications, other CRM) means we can build models to score our users based on the funnel events they have reacted to. Using organic versus paid gives us a better understanding of the level of engagement and the clarity surrounding our product and its use. Usually, organic users will be more engaged with our product as

USER SCORING 51

we did not pay to lead them to using us, but this is not always the case.

As we continue to work with this type of scoring, we can create user profiles and decide what we wish to do with them based on their interaction with us; do we wish to keep advertising re-engagement campaigns, or do we wish to keep them in the cold without investing further capital? We can decide what type of content we send them: educational, awareness, or none.

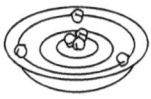

When you run a hummus restaurant, you don't wish to be famous for your shakshuka. You advertise yourself as a hummus place — with the goal of selling all the hummus by the end of each day, since it needs to be made fresh daily. But instead of hummus, your customers keep coming to consume your falafel and shakshuka; the product you need to sell the most is not moving anywhere! There's a problem. You can start advertising your hummus, and some may pass your restaurant up, but others come in and sit down; great! Now you offer them a taste of your hummus, but they leave without buying. What happened? Did you do something wrong? Is the hummus bad? Like this restaurant experience, setting your funnel steps and understanding what you must change to increase sales conversions helps improve the quality of guests walking through your door.

Incidentally, a campaign that brings us low-scoring users shouldn't have more money thrown at it; rather, it should be optimized. If that doesn't lead to higher scores, *then stop pumping money into it.*

If we see that people aren't using — or responding to — features, there's likely a product issue that requires a re-design and subsequent consumer re-education. Their "trip down the funnel" should show us the places we want them to explore before they arrive at the destination: conversion. Grading their progress is best accomplished by a model where each step represents a percentage of an overall score of 100%; the model should be dynamic and adaptable based on what we learn about our user's journey.

Let's start this model with an assumption in terms of how we think the user should use our product. What are the touch points we designed to convince him to convert? From there, we can track his activity, and the more data we capture, the more evidence we must test if our assumptions were right. After the first 1,000 visits (why 1,000? Just a fixed number to have enough traffic to work with), it's likely we'll see some trends we can use to learn if our design flow is correct — or needs adaptation. We'll see if they follow the funnel we designed, if we need to try another one, or whether it's worth our effort.

After we've fixed our assumptions regarding the funnel, it's important to review the importance of each step, creating new assumptions about the most important event for the conversion. What's least important (regarding the conversion's golden event) and what is more important? I usually use sticky notes for the breakdown:

20%	Add to cart	10%
18%	Watched product	10%
12%	Land on home page	5%
10%		5%
10%		5%
		5%

USER SCORING

In this stage, it's vital to understand that we need to create *several flows*, i.e., new users landing on the site, organic users, paid users, returning users from CRM, paid channel, etc. Each type in this flow will have different patterns; you should be able to understand them. *NOTE: Depending upon the country and the mobile device, there will be different patterns.*

While many may say this is not the most conventional way to track users (and possibly, a bit unethical), it's important to data-centricity to measure how the users are interacting with the platform — what they are doing, and do they take funnel steps in the way for which we designed the funnel to be most effective?

With the new privacy laws and less visibility in terms of our users, each user funnel we can track becomes gold! In this age, where data availability has is key to company survival, the only companies rising above the fray will be those able to understand their users, growing from opt-ins and tracking — and an immediate ability to improve the app when needed.

Work on your user scoring today. Build your assumptions, update them each time you change something, and confirm that your scoring system is relevant. Using this model for just three months, you can adapt it more closely based on real numbers, approaching a reality dynamic by measuring users' interaction with each step, arriving at more likelihood of them to convert. The more historic data you have, the more accurate your model will become; in a year's time, you'll be able to use if for forecasting revenue and setting goals for the marketing team.

Becoming More Data-Centric

When I first met Gerrit, Bri, and Lore, I understood that they needed to become less dependent upon their individual data strategies and learn to rely more on team strategies while allowing each to have their own data.

You'll see, below, that the concept I had for transforming this team is centered on focusing on *actions instead of data*. I learned this from watching many organizations that concentrated on the collection of data rather than *understanding how to use the data to drive decisions* (or action). Too often, the big question was glossed over (*why am I using this data?*) and instead ended up with a lot of KPIs, confusion, and poor decisions. So, we all learned that the

best motivator for using data wasn't the amassing great quantities, it was it gathering the right data, understanding how to use it to form structured decision trees — all while maintaining control over that data.

In these sections, we'll learn how to drive a data discovery workshop, going over your data deeply to define what is important (and what isn't), how to create documentation for your BI person in terms of the best way to run analyses on your data. I'll also talk about the important role ROI has in terms of your daily decisions.

Everything I share is knowledge gained (and refined) by working with different teams within different companies, understanding that each team is different. Still, we all faced the same challenge, which brought me to creating the tunnel you'll see below.

It's important to keep in mind the difference between reporting and analysis, while reporting is predefined and set by the data consumer to make quick and easy decisions, analysis should investigate and explain a phenomenon that the reports can't explain. In the workshop, we will focus on reporting, and afterwards we will explain how to do meaningful analysis.

The Data Discovery Workshop (DDW)

Talking with Gerrit, Bri, and Lore, I understood that we needed to have more structure with our data, but it wasn't enough just to *have it*, we had to understand it and define the processes that drove quick reactions/easy decisions. This approach was much more effective than the long, complex set of systems where each team member had his own path, and then had to *meld his scheme with others' schemes.*

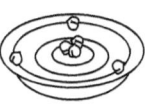

My daughter is only a year old, but she is already going crazy for hummus! She loves it so much that we created an Index after her name; if her plate contains hummus and something else, and after one spoonful of hummus she returns to something else on her plate, the hummus is bad. If she asks for more hummus after the first spoonful, we have a rising star! If she jumps from her chair toward the plate, we have a clear winner! In Israel, we can list two places she jumped out of her chair, Halil Restaurant in Ramla, and Abu Shukri in Haifa.

The DDW has two main functions:

1. **Clarity about decision making** — As a team, we need to define what is important for us and how we wish to make decisions. We'll create a detailed document about decision-making in the workshop.

2. **Clear data strategy** — We will design our data strategy, focusing on what's most important. Providing BI with a clear strategy is the first step in making our goals a reality.

We need to move away from "big data" into the world of "data product," creating a clear roadmap for ourselves and for our engineers. For the BI, this is no longer a project they need to finish; it's a product that needs to be maintained — and supervised — on a constant basis. The workshop is designed to act as a funnel; in each step, we reduce data noise, we define measures, dimensions, and KPIs, driving clarity and transforming the team into a "data product" mindset.

What should you prepare for the workshop?

- A comfortably sized room for all participants
- Seats and tables with plenty of room to write
- Pick your participants carefully with their direct effect on the team
- Whiteboard and whiteboard markers
- Black markers for each participant
- Sticky notes (three colors, minimum)
- Sticker dots in two colors
- Sugary things — trust me, you will need them!
- A0 prints of the following views (size is 841 × 1189 mm, or 33.1 × 46.8 inches)

What are the rules?

- **Four hours — NO longer!** Use your time wisely; if it's too short, you've missed something important. If it's too long, you are likely out of focus. However, the *first* time may take longer, but learn from it and improve as a team. Your focus should be on driving actions. If a decision can't be made, it should sidelined so that proper communication can take place, where team members can lay down arguments. How? We'll discuss that a little later.

- **Break it into three sessions** — Three sessions with 15-minute breaks works well, but I've often used just one break, saving the extra time for Question/Answer or time to work through clearing any hurdles we've discovered.

- **No computers/mobile phones** — Four hours without laptops or cells will keep everyone focused on designing the data product. The sky won't fall in four hours...dedicate this time to the project at hand.

- **No judging** — The session should be open, allowing anyone to raise concerns or thoughts, as long as the focus remains on the quality of the data and decision-making.

- **Dare to dream** — The design you arrive at during the workshop should not be related to what you have or don't have *today*. Everything is on the table; anything can be considered — allow yourself to dream!

- **Keep it moderated** — Don't slow down, don't lose track. Set one moderator in the room who oversees governing the process, who can decide what is relevant or less relevant for the sessions, and who keeps everyone focused, and it's not your lead.

- **Take pictures** — It's important that each stage of the workshop will be recorded, not in video but with pictures, you don't need to photo the participants but the Post-it notes in each stage, take pictures of the way you grouped or work on each stage so you remember the logic you used.

Preparations Before the Session

- **Synopsis** — Create a dedicated shared document which participants follow and make room for notetaking. This keeps the conversation efficient.

- **The department's key players** — Who are the people in the department, what are their specific roles, and how do they relate to the process you are building?

- **Outline your data** — Map all your data sources. It doesn't matter if you are downloading it directly or downloading via a third party; list them all. For example, if you get attribution data from Google, it goes on the list.

- **Outline your issues** — Map today's issues, from data from not arriving on time (and *when* you should be getting it) to the level of details needed. It's also important for data engineers to know today's issues.

- **Outline Scrutiny** — How is your team being measured? What do you need to deliver? If working in products, do you measure success by increasing the use of features? If you're in marketing, is your yardstick returning users or converting more users into sales? Scrutinize goals and numbers, putting them in writing.

- **Infrastructure outlay** — What is the infrastructure and tools you are employing *today*? Write this down, including where and how you store your data; if you aren't certain, ask the BI team to send you the structure of their process.

- **Your purpose** — Every team should have a purpose; what's yours? How do you use data to achieve your purpose, what is working well with the data you use and what are you missing to get a better understanding over the situation, write it down in big letters, make sure it's clear and agreed by you and the team.

First session — Get to know your data

Session time: 45—60 minutes
What will be used: Post-it notes (two colors), markers, dot stickers (in two colors.)

The first session involves a lot of exploration: Why do we need the data? What data do we believe is required? What are the questions — or doubts — that teams have in terms of the system in place today? Remember to dream! How would the best reporting LOOK? Put everything on the table and let everyone speak up. try to avoid specific KPIs, but more forming questions. Speaking of table...

A round-table format is best. Get permission (in advance) from the department lead to allow someone else to moderate and become part of the team. Flat hierarchy ensures more openness from participants and precipitates a good flow of questions. Leave your opinion outside of the room, leave data issues at the door (aside from simple assessment) and commit to giving serious thought to what you need to make yourself successful in running the business.

It's crucial that the moderator decide (in advance) the function of each Post-it color; one color should indicate questions regarding KPIs, the other should indicate general questions regarding tools and methods.

At the round table, allow each member to stick a Post-it on the wall, beginning clockwise. The Post-it should include questions that the member has regarding his own data view (what he need or wishes to see) and regarding tools and methods used by the team. Each participant will write their notes and read them aloud to the team and allowing time for clarifications. This keeps the questions at the forefront, keeps the conversation lively, and avoids duplicate questions.

As a moderator, the important part for him will be to challenge the team to think outside of the comfort zone, raise directions not on the wall and maybe offer a direction not taken; it's important to make sure we think outside of the box during the session.

The two dots will define better general questions we need to focus on and some that can be left for a later stage, what we will do with it is to mark top important questions, even before we are voting on them.

Data Discovery workshop canvas (Session 1.1)

| How many installs we drive each day? | What is the average length of a session? | What are our top rated partners? | What is the gereral path of a user? | What is the first menu item being clicked? | Using CPI is the right thing? | How long can we store a user information? |

| Is Firebase the tool for us? | Are we sure our revenue forecast is correct? |

KPIs related questions
(limited to 15)

General questions
(limited to 15)

Using the 2-color dot stickers, keep the questions in two categories: Require more thinking, and clear for conversation questions. Avoid questions like "Does it make sense to do affiliate marketing?", instead focusing on narrower questions, such as "Is affiliate marketing working better then display partners?" A few more examples of good questions:

- Is using Google Firebase for attribution data the right way to go?
- How many installs do we generate per day?
- How much does my department spend per day?
- Which country drives best ROI?
- How many active users do we have daily?
- How do define "session"?
- Should we use ROI forecasts?

BECOMING MORE DATA-CENTRIC 61

Less productive questions might look like:
- Why do we use attribution tool A?
- How much do we pay for data storage?

Give yourself and the team 45 minutes to raise questions around the entire table, allowing participants to pass if they have no question. Continue until there are no more questions or the 45-minutes is up.

Now, take 10 minutes to let each member of the team to vote for the questions he think are most relevant for him/team; simply make a mark on each note for each vote. Members can only vote once per Post-it but are unlimited as to the number of different notes on which to vote.

After the voting is over, the moderator should form new two columns on the wallboard; one for KPI-related questions, the other for general questions, arranging those in descending order based on the most-votes-per-Post-it question. Limit the number to 40, total. Questions not making this list will be discussed in the next part of the workshop.

The general questions will not be part of the process we are about to do in the workshop; you can keep them on the wall, you can put them down, but you need to keep them *for after the workshop.*

Data Discovery workshop canvas   (Session 1.3)

	What is the average ength of a session?	What are our top rated partners?	What is the gereral path of a user?		How long can we store a user information?
	Are we sure our revenue forecast is correct?				

KPIs related questions (limited to 15)	How many installs we drive each day?	What is the first menu item being clicked?		
General questions (limited to 15)	Is Firebase the tool for us?	Using CPI is the right thing?		

Break time

Break time: 15 minutes

Use the time to review the tickets again, use the restroom, get some air, etc., but not laptops or cellphones yet, please!

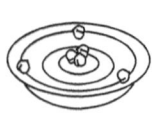

In Israel, sometimes hummus is regarded as a second religion. Every Friday, you will see the hummus places fully packed and people waiting in lines to get through the door. Waiting only makes you hungry, as you watch the people sitting at tables full of food, and when you finally get to your seat, there isn't much time for thinking; you'll need to know what you want. You may have strangers at your table — sharing the love of hummus — but there's little time for talk, as you'll be expected to leave as soon as your plate is finished. Don't take too much time taking pictures of your plate; instead focus on the amazing dish and enjoy every moment eating it.

Second session — Design Your Data

Session time: 50–70 minutes
What will be used: Post-it notes (different color than the previous sessions) and markers.

Entering this phase, we are reminded to "Keep the WHY", using our time to focus on the questions related to KPIs. In this session, we hope to create a map of our measures and dimensions required for analysis or decision-making.

Since time is limited, take 20-30 minutes to go over each KPI-related question, start with the ones with the highest votes, and try to group them, each member suggesting relevant dimension/s and measure/s that he/she believe are most important to the process — and WHY.

Everything discussed should be within the reference of WHY. This ensures that we aren't adding irrelevant conjecture into the session, especially into the part where members are explaining why they believe their approach is relevant. This is not the time to discuss conflicts, but instead, raise pertinent questions regarding an existing problem (which later needs to be structured more thoughtfully.) You can use the stickers from the previous session to mark them.

Don't add measures or dimensions which are not related to the questions on board (we will have time for it in a later stage), and please keep things focused on the questions ahead.

Data Discovery workshop canvas   (Session 2.1)

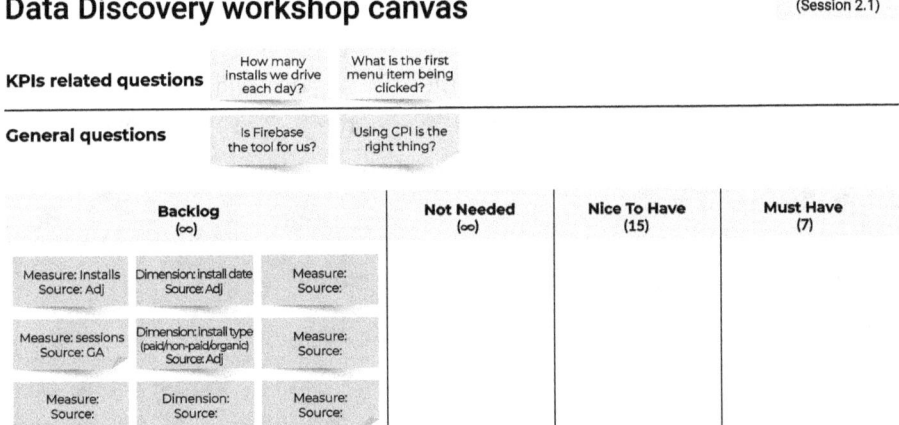

KPI-related questions

To clarify, participants will consider each question, writing down the measures (don't talk KPIs just yet) that they think are relevant to the answer — as well as the dimensions. Encourage them to focus on the measures, NOT the calculation (KPI). For example, if you wish to know the ROI — which is a KPI — you will need to measure first costs, then revenues. We will deal with KPIs in the third part of the session.

For example:

- *How many daily installs do I have?*
    - The answer involves a measure (which is installs) and dimension of date, so we can see the installs daily. If we see a drop in installs for a few days, perhaps our campaigns have lost scalability, or maybe our tracking has been compromised.
- *What is the average length of a session?*
    - To arrive at this answer, we'll need sessions, session time, and timestamps. We wish to arrive at an average of all sessions, so if we see a drop in session times, we'll know we may have an issue with the site.

For each of the measures or dimensions you will include in this section, you will need to add the source. Do you take install information from Google Firebase, or are you using a third-party attribution tool?

"How many installs do I have on a daily basis?"

Drive sub-questions from this ticket, such as:

- What source am I using to track installs? To form one true source, do I use attribution tools or internal count of new devices?
- What is an install? Is it complete after the first session? Am I including devices that had a *reinstall* in the count of installs? How many days should pass between the first install and a second install to be counted as a "new install"?
- Date of install: Is that the install date by the attribution provider, or the date in our system?

These questions — and more — will help us to define the measure as "installs"; however, now we need to define the source of it. Is it coming from Google Firebase, Adjust, Appsflyer, or another attribution tool? We answer these questions to establish the one true source for the number of installs, aligning the team on which number should they use.

Continue in this way (questions/answers) until all the KPI-related questions on the board are covered, being sure that the moderator raises sub-questions, allowing the team to answer, and placing everything on the board into backlog.

When you finish, and have enough measures and dimensions on the board, look at the dimensions. We can already say that we wish to see "date" and to be able to filter by it, but there are other dimensions to consider. Do we wish to know if this is paid install or if it is organic? Do we wish to know where the user came from in terms of country, region, and city? These additional questions complete our dimensions quickly. Add them on a separate Post-it color, so you will remember that they external to the processes you did, and *not linked to the question*. This provides us with a greater slice of our data to launch better decisions.

General questions

General questions have no real place in our workshop, as we wish to design the strategy, working quickly on it. We will need to facilitate the conversation for each of the tickets by setting working teams or responsible people. When I work on these subjects, I like to add them all into tickets and then into a Word or Google docs file which I can share with the rest of the team. I set a clear timeline for dealing with each question starting with the highest voted subjects and taking it slowly down to the less important.

We do want to talk about general questions eventually, but they may require more thinking and learning before we can deal with them.

General questions cannot be answered quickly, so if these exist, assign them to a person who will arrive at least two solutions for each, documenting those inside the file. The idea is to kick up more conversation later and come up with a team outcome. For example, questions such as: "Is it smart to use a CPA for campaign optimization?" This is a valid question, and the team should ask whether this is an issue for them. Later, in the document, the team will offer how it is a problem, as well as how to approach and correct the issue. At the next workshop, you'll be able to refer to these questions, tracking changes and the current status.

General question	Solution offered 1	Solution offered 2	Risks
Is Affiliate marketing working better for us than paid marketing?	We will set an A/B test between the two...		

Sorting the columns

If your prior sessions were successful, you should now have a backlog full of measures and dimensions, remembering your KPIs, so now you can start sorting the measures into columns of "Nice to have", "Must have", and "Not needed."

Each measure should garner careful thought from each member in the room. Is this a "must have?" For instance, installs are a MUST for your business in order to measure the success of the app. It would be nice to know how many of those installs have uploaded a profile image, but that's not crucial as a KPI; still, it's a helpful indicator. Clear your backlog from all the measures and leave only the dimensions in the backlog.

Be certain to rank high-value measures at the top so you have clear visual cues in terms of most important and least important.

Data Discovery workshop canvas   (Session 2.2.2)

KPIs related questions	How many installs we drive each day?	What is the first menu item being clicked?
General questions	Is Firebase the tool for us?	Using CPI is the right thing?

Backlog (∞)	Not Needed (∞)	Nice To Have (15)	Must Have (7)
Measure: sessions Source: GA	Dimension: install type (paid/non-paid/organic) Source: Adj	Measure: Source:	Measure: Installs Source: Adj
	Measure: Source:	Dimension: Source:	Dimension: install date Source: Adj
		Measure: Source:	Measure: Source:

Break time

Break time: 15 minutes

Use the time to review the tickets again, use the restroom, get some air, etc., but not laptops or cellphones yet, please!

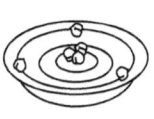

> *A moment of joy:* the moment you arrive at your hummus restaurant, the server already knows what you like. He welcomes you with a smile, seats you like you are a VIP, and then the dish arrives at your table within moments of your arrival! Just 15 minutes from the moment you entered, you are already out the door, full and happy.

Third session — The Visualizations

Session time: 60–90 minutes
What will be used: Post-it notes (different color from previous sessions) and markers.

Congratulations! Your teams have arrived at the last part of the workshop. Let's reduce our funnel one level lower, focusing on which data drives actions, designing the visualizations and reporting, and how that reporting system looks.

The measures we have prepared in Session 2 will go onto a new white board, constructed in two columns, allowing us to now build up the required KPIs for our process. Be aware that the dimensions will need to be limited; if you have ten or more dimensions, make sure they are the *most important ones!*

Data Discovery workshop canvas   (Session 3.2)

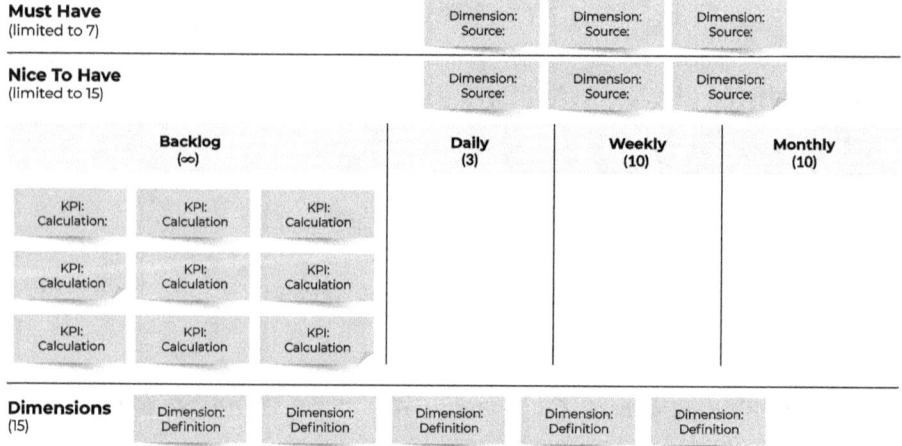

Populating the Backlog

Start by distinguishing which measures need a number, such as installs, sessions, and measures. We are creating tickets for them, storing those in the backlog; notice that the backlog is limited.

After we set the measures we will need for an efficient database, it's time to set our KPIs based on them. Your team needs to consider, for example, if your ROI is an important factor. If so, what measures must be used for it? Revenue, revenue forecasts, "costs -1", or some other calculation? Each KPI that lands on the backlog should have the name, the source, and how this calculation is processed. Keep creating these KPIs, adding them to the backlog.

Reporting

Before jumping into the subject of building up reporting, we should just set some lines of work and how the last phase of your workshop should appear. Overflows of data or overpopulated reports are to be avoided — as is the love of Excel! Let's avoid those issues, centering our attention on what's important, rather than wasting time on irrelevant information.

Our reports should *drive actions*. If no action comes from our reports in two weeks, STOP, rethink the KPIs you are using. This report should be built by the decision-maker himself, creating weekly reports for deep dives and investigations; a monthly report can reflect on the decision made, and show how aligned — or unaligned — we were with management's targets.

Going into the last stage, we need to make sure we are aligning with the team and company targets, understanding the way we are being measured, and understanding we just cannot use over three KPIs to make our decisions — because using more than three means we can't make decisions! Either you say you are creating a user scoring, or measuring against ROI N (or only feature conversion); this is up to you and management to decide, but the goal is to make sure that *your daily reports are aligned with your goals.*

Our reports should **drive action.** If you can't decide based on your data — and this happens two weeks in a row — you've done something wrong, and it's time to repeat the workshop. In his book, The Art of War, Sun Tzu said, "The general who wins the battle makes many calculations in his temple before the battle is fought. The general who loses makes but few calculations beforehand." This is our exact goal when we build our reports infrastructure: first, we learn about ourselves and our data to drive better actions.

To enable us to consume data with minimum noise, we need to split our tables and processes into three categories, each being a standalone process to secure our actions and understanding of the data.

The daily report — decision's report Is the most important report we will build. It allows us to make quick and easy decisions, it's the report with the least KPIs (up to 3 KPIs only), and its goal is to tell you if you are working correctly or not. Once we get this report in the morning, we immediately know what needs to be done, we know what is working — and what requires our attention. A good report provides the right dimensions/filters for the data consumer to delve into as deeply as he can to understand the issues, providing a quick reflection of the daily activity.

The weekly report — Review decisions is supplied on Monday mornings, providing an overview of up to 10 KPIs and showing the general direction we are headed: Have we made good decisions during the daily optimization?   Do our product features deliver needed conversions?   This report provides support to analyze daily activity and benchmark it against the past. Think of it as the map to either support or contradict your decisions.

The monthly report helps us tell our story to stakeholders, managers, and team members, as we are being measured against a target, *and those people want to know if we're measuring up.* This report explains the direction we chose — and the direction we took — during the past month, providing a full overview of all activity.

The key to designing a good report is asking the right questions, which can lead to better performance. Having the right numbers — numbers aligned from the CEO level to the lowest-level employee — will help management ask the right questions, help employees know what the company goals are, and synchronize the team agenda.

The job of the reports is to clear the way for making good decisions. You create a fixed structure that changes once each quarter (if needed), always using the same set of KPIs so that you can spot changes easily and have consistency over the decisions. On the other side, analysis requires time and planning. The key to effective analysis is diving deep into a subject you don't see daily, which may explain a change of user behavior. Analysis shouldn't be undertaken on a daily or weekly schedule, as daily and weekly reports should contain most of your answers.

Dimensions

Dimensions (15) | Dimension: Definition | Dimension: Definition | Dimension: Definition | Dimension: Definition | Dimension: Definition

When we design our tables, we wish to set a limit to the filters/segmentations we are using. We have the basic ones — such as date, GEO, and marketing campaign information — but next to each of them, we need to identify the source of the data and the level of the details we wish to consider. For each of Post-it we had in the "Nice-to-have "and the "Must-have" columns, we will add the dimensions that can be driven by these questions.

For example, if we have a question about how many installs each ad partner delivered each day, we can already say we will need a partner dimension and a data dimension based on installs.

After finishing this one, take the time to think about filters or dimensions you think are relevant, populating the backlog with questions such as:

- If you design a cohort table, what should be the anchor date? For example, is it the install date or the session date? How many days ahead should the cohorts go?
- What level of the campaign are we presenting? Is it staying on the campaign level or going as deep as the creative/keyword level?
- Do we need to have a split between new users and returning users? How do we segment our users?

Each question should create a ticket that will later be a dimension, but make sure each dimension picked is *relevant for the task at hand*. (See Chart Below)

Dimension: the names of the dimensions are written here.

Definition: new users reflected in a first-time site visit, returning users have returned the second time within the first 14 days from the first visit.

This should be very clear to anyone using this report.

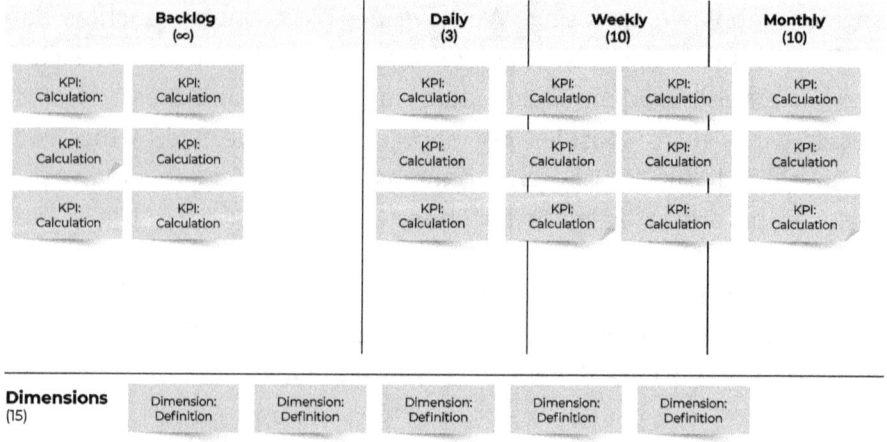

Creating the reports

After creating the backlog, we begin with the KPIs, allowing each team member to vote for the tickets. Use about 10 minutes for this process, then begin organizing the KPIs with the highest votes on the right top side of your backlog.

Now, time to populate the reports, creating three reports focused on decision-making and using actionable data.

Daily

The daily report is limited to 3 KPIs and is focused on actions we need to drive each day (such as campaign optimization), and its goal is focusing on the most important information in terms of actionable decisions.

For example, a new measure (campaign ranking) may include several measures and weights to indicate the quality of the campaigns; based on this this, you can decide if the campaign is working well or not.

Weekly

The weekly report is limited to 10 KPIs, each selected to clarify decisions we have made during the week. If our main decision KPI is campaign ranking, we can include several highly weighted KPIs used for the calculation, allowing us to judge if the model is correct or not. Again, this should be focused on actionable data; if a KPI doesn't drive action, there is no reason to include it here.

Monthly

Like the weekly report, the monthly report is limited to 10 KPIs and is used by the team to communicate with the management team, explaining actions and showing performance against the company targets. Likewise, it provides a way for team leads to arrive at a better overview of the team's health and performance using these KPIs.

Overall, this report should be fixed and adapted only once every three months for checking the quality and the relevancy of the tables and reports.

Conclude the workshop

Great job! Now you have formed the first outlay of your data strategy; now it's time to start the second part: ticket creation for the data engineer. *This process is not less important than the first!*

The workshop showed us what we need to have and what questions to answer, but after we finished, we cannot simply pin the result on the wall and forget about it. We must create a document that includes all the things we've discussed, explaining the order chosen and why we picked what we picked.

We must create tickets for the data engineers in terms of what we need, the format, and the source. This document will be used internally, but it will be based on important factors such as the privacy policy, explaining why we collect the data and what we do with it.

Your workshop outcomes should be used for a full three months before you change them. Why? Because that much time should be allowed for the data engineers to stabilize the process (and for yourself to use it and get accustomed to using it), identifying the issues and challenges in the structure you have created.

Finding your comfort zone is important, and after you have completed three months of working the data, you'll be smarter in the way you work with it. Don't give up on the process too soon; this is the only way to become decision-driven, saving time in the future.

The general questions are important; review them and assign the right member in your team to deal with them and share the results. Keep it running for three months so in the next workshop, you will arrive with some having learned new directions, and will be prepared to drive better data strategy out of the entire process.

One more important point: automate your reporting with some software such as Tableau, Power BI, or another you like, putting it into use early. Also, unless it's for analysis, stop using Excel.

Creating Tickets for Data Engineers

Mapping the sources. Once we have a roadmap and decide on a strategy, it's time to create request tickets for the data engineer. At this stage, it's important that we will have all the required resources of the team and are fully engaged with the project.

Creating a basic database and APIs shouldn't take your data engineering team longer than three weeks *if you created the right tickets with a clear strategy and priority list.* To write the tickets correctly, start with the second session where the dimensions, measures, and sources of this data have been identified; we need not go into the calculation of KPIs at this stage.

Your data engineer should start by downloading all the available information from the third-party source using an API, storing it in a place where you have access. Even if you didn't ask for that access, it's always good to have it in the long-term, and the data engineer should set a daily download of ALL data into the raw level daily. It's important to download EVERYTHING; perhaps, in three months, you may require different data, but most sources usually delete historical data after several days. Fetching the data in the lowest and widest way into your database will ensure you have it all when you need it. Remember to QA it against the third-party dashboards you are using.

After you have finished your QA, the data engineer can build the first standardized/aggregated tables, allowing you to QA it once again, making sure the data is correct. Each step should be with a feedback loop between you and the engineer to ensure that the information you provided is being used correctly.

Creating the Documentation

This document creates an overview of the databases and sources required by the team. In the following pages, we will outline the sources of data and the aggregated tables we need to simplify our decision-making processes.

During the workshop, we have identified the data sources, the measures, dimensions, and KPIs we will require in achieving our goal of _____ (*fill in your mission and goal*). We want to drive a clear and fast process, so we create an outline of our requirements.

How to make this document successful?

This is just a kick-off document, and as such, we need to stimulate data sharing.

1. Fill any gaps with data sources that need to be connected.
2. Add comments next to dimensions and measures if you think the description is wrong.
3. Mark with color if the dimensions and measures are available (● = existing, □ = need to check, ○ = need to be created).
4. Add your views regarding the final tables, visualizing the end-product.
5. If you find a mistake or think something is missing, add it on the last page in the designated area: "**Conversation mistakes, vision, and comments.**"

 *When I first went to my first hummus preparation course — hoping to learn the best techniques for tasty dishes — I thought it was, surely, all about the type of chickpeas, tahini, or water you use. Instead, I was told it's about how you build the layers of taste and the balance between them. The hummus, the oil, the chickpeas, and the spices need to mix in each bite, leaving a good aftertaste to usher in the next bite.*

Data Sources

To simplify, we need to map all the data sources from the workshop into an easy-to-read table. Next to it, we should also add whether it's available on the DWH of the company, so the data engineers will know what is required of them.

Source	Type	Source aggregator	Availability	Comments
Adjust	Mobile attribution	Direct download	◐	
Google Analytics	Web attribution	Direct download	◐	Stored on BigQuery for now
Amazon	Ad Partner	Funnel.io	☐	
Google Ads	Ad Partner	Funnel.io	☐	
Youtube	Ad Partner	Funnel.io	☐	
Apple Search Ads	Ad Partner	Funnel.io	☐	
Audience Network	Ad Partner	Funnel.io	☐	

◐ = available on DWH   ☐ = Not available on DWH   ○ = need to build API

Definition

Now let's define some essential points. For example, how do we identify a "session"? What is an "install"? Even: what is an "ad partner"? It's important to document it here, so we have it for any future workshop or development, and this will be the referring point to any new team member.

Session — A session starts when a user opens the app or website, which is longer than ten seconds; the session ends when the user zooms out or closes the window.

Reach — Combination of the first install of the app (the user downloaded and had the first session) AND first session (without cookie) on the site.

Tables outlay

Here, we are focusing on the daily, weekly, and monthly tables we have designed in our data discovery workshop. Starting with the daily table first, we have the dimensions and measures already structured in the aggregated level data, so this stage should be simple.

We want to create a map of the last part of our workshop, the reporting, for the daily, weekly and monthly tables, explaining the dimensions, KPIs, and measures required, and mapping them all into dimension groups, descriptions, sources, and examples of how it should look.

If you are not sure about a few points, always ask your data engineer for his input, finding the best solutions to make it happen.

CREATING TICKETS FOR DATA ENGINEERS

Dimension Group	Dimensions	Description	Data Source	Example	Availability
Date	Session date	The data session created	Events	YYYY-MM-DD	
General	Platform	The source of the event Web/App	Attribution	Web App	
	User Segmentation	What type of user is it coming after registration	Event?	Student Divorced	
	App version	What app version the event belongs to	Attribution	2.2.1	
	OS	The OS used to create a session for the user	Attribution	IOS Android Chrome	
	Device	The device brand	Attribution	iPhone Samsung	

● = available on DWH   = Not available on DWH   = need to build API

Measure	Description	DataSource	The parameter name (internal)	Calculation	Availability?
ROI Forecast	Revenue forecast based on the model divided by the accumulated costs	Revenue	ROI FC	Revenue/Costs - 1 = ##.#%	
Reached	The total new users landed on the web/app on day X	Attribution	Reached	Installs + new web users	
Campaign Scoring	The score each campaign receives based on the formula				

Mapping aggregated tables

Map your aggregated data into several tables. Each will have a different function, but it's important that you have them all placed in a level people can access.

1. **Attribution table** — This is based on session-level information and should contain the session and the events created, and the source of the session, if applicable.

2. **User Table** — Each user you have engaged with should have a unique identification in this, and each identification should list the events that have happened for the device. For example, in the case of revenues, the table should include accumulated revenue, or any other important event based on the 23 KPIs you picked during the last step of our data discovery workshop.

3. **Costs table** — This table tracks costs on the lowest level possible with the campaign metadata and the amount spent, including the results, such as installs, registration, reinstalls, and more.

4. **Events table** — This table captures events that were tracked in the system, with the device that drove the event and the event name; the more information you have, the better.

5. Try to keep one key across all these tables — which should be the **user identification ID**.

Having the data structured in this way will ensure the ability of the different teams to consume the data if required, and — when needed — to run an analysis of the data. In this way, you know you have the rawest level of data to learn from.

Each table design should be broken down into small sprints (two weeks each), where X amount of KPIs and measures are done, until we have it all constructed. If the data engineer can't deliver useable tables in two weeks, we are facing an issue that needs to be fixed. We cannot wait three months to have data; by that time, nothing would be relevant. When each sprint is finished, kick the tables to the team to QA and learn about the data, making sure it is correct.

No EXCEL

Excel is one of the biggest downfalls for organizations. We need data now, fast and dirty, and many don't trust their database's data, so they turn to Excel. For years, I tried to enforce the "NO Excel" policy so that all data arrived from the database, enabling teams to consume what they needed when they needed it.

Often, I have distributed an Excel sheet just to discover (afterward) a huge mistake with the VLookup, or that something else in my process was broken. After sending the incorrect information to 300 people in the organization, I had to send out an apology email, asking the data consumers not to use the Excel sheet I just sent. This created delays for other teams, and if you've experienced this, you already know how disrupting and time-consuming it can be to correct the situation.

This experience taught me that Excel should be abolished inside of organizations, being replaced with a state-of-the-art reporting system connected directly to databases prepared in advance to using analysis. The databases should be checked daily so that if changes occur, an update can be made automatically. This kind of system helps us all become more efficient, as all teams are using the same one true source (built by a computer) and avoiding human error in terms of calculation mistakes.

The "NO Excel" policy ensures that each time a team requires a report, a data guy sits with them, understanding their goals and the data they use, and creating an alternative to Excel. Foregoing the use of Excel also means we don't waste time in preparing our report; we no longer have to refresh the Excel sheet by bringing in all the sources into different tables, running the VLookups, checking to make sure they make sense, and wasting even more time trying to correct the links. These processes can take hours — sometimes even days — of work time. And if the reports use Java to collect and process the data, then you need to wait for someone who knows how to fix it; *just don't go there.*

The last problem with Excel is the data manipulation we tend to do, sometimes not even aware of it, but still, it happens. I call it "beautification of results" because no one wants to reveal poor results, so people often filter out data that doesn't fit their agenda.

On top of it all, you not always aware of data limitations (something your data engineer will know best), so if you are planning to become a data-centric, ditch Excel and use pre-fixed databases. Or, you can use your data engineer to help you get your data (if it's out of the data scoop at this moment), and he can also doublecheck to make sure the data is reliable and can be used for decisions.

Applying the policy in your company will help people get used to reducing data noise and become more focused on what they wish to achieve (decision-making), rather than running around like a headless chicken without the ability to make simple decisions!

Analysis — The Right Way

We have talked about reports and how to structure them, and now it's time to consider *analysis*, another part of using data, but a part that causes a lot of chaos and noise — which must be reduced. Analysis usually needs to follow a question and assumption that is invisible on reports and needing further investigation, but it's not usually worth adding it to our daily reports. We need to pull some data and run the analysis on it.

Unfortunately, *unnecessary analysis* is your organization's biggest problem! Often, we're asked to build analysis with no clear outcome. Why do you need to know the share of furniture versus computers sold online in the past few months?

How many of you have extracted data or run an analysis, just leaving it there, never looking at it again? I found a way to avoid performing nonessential analysis.

First things first: analysis requests shouldn't be made until a simple form is filled out and tracked in a centralized place; this protects us from repeated analysis. Once, I overhead an analyst talking to his team lead during lunch break. He was complaining about the CEO's fifth request for him to run an analysis that month, but the CEO didn't explain what he did with the data, or what he wished to discover; this is wrong in so many ways!

Running analysis should help us to understand something we can't find in the reports, but if it's becoming a weekly thing, then it should go on the reports. Clearly, it has some impact on the business.

To make sure we avoid extra work in terms of analysis (again, assumptions to drive actions), we need to start with creating a template where the organization's daily, weekly, monthly, and ad hoc questions can be listed. Why do we do it? Because sometimes, people will look and find that the data they need is already in a report, saving wasted hours of writing a ticket and driving our analyst crazy in extracting the data. (I love using a tool such as Asana/Trello for this purpose.)

I suggest adding all the daily, weekly, and monthly questions in an organized way so that if someone searches for keywords, he will find his answers more easily. I add labels showing who each report belongs to, and I also add the dimensions the report contains. This way, a lot of information is already provided to the person searching for the analysis.

Finally, I add a column with the most recent analysis done in the company, usually leaving a 30-day window of analysis. Anything older is archived — but still available if searched — and in this way, people can see if something was already done, and can either ask for it or contact the person requesting the report.

If the requester can't find what he is searching for, he can create a new ticket. Such a ticket should explain the rationale behind the analysis request, the assumption, and what outcome he wishes to have with the data.

Such tickets should include these details:
   a. Name
   b. Department
   c. Priority
   d. Money value, if available, *if it impacts investments or monetary decisions*
   e. Status (pending, in progress, QA'ed, in review by the requester, finished)

The data consumer should provide the background in terms of requesting the analysis, i.e., what led him to request the data, as well as outlining the method he wishes to use in the report, what numbers or dimensions, as well as if he wishes them to be calculated in a certain way. To conclude, the requester should end his ticket

ANALYSIS — THE RIGHT WAY

with the results expected based on the data — specifically, what he will do if his assumptions are proven to be right.

A fully developed ticket ensures that the analyst understands what is expected from him; if he sees more relevant data during his research, he can mention it in the output. The data extractor then needs to save his queries and results (in case they are needed inside the ticket or internal system), for 30 days before he archives or deletes them due to *perceived* irrelevance.

- **Background**: Although we observe an increase in Swedish traffic on Facebook, we do not see an increase in the number of conversions, and we wish to understand why.
- **The method:** By comparing the conversion funnel score for this source against that for other traffic sources, we decide to allocate more funding for Facebook Sweden.
- **Results**: After performing our analysis using a Facebook tracker, we see that the issue has been resolved, and the Facebook numbers are back to normal.

Following this method will allow you to focus on actions, obtain meaningful information, and create feedback loops that will eliminate useless performance analysis.

Many will say they don't have time for all these details (especially CEOs who must deal with 50 other things simultaneously) but forcing it as part of the culture will ensure the company becomes data-efficient *and data-centric*.

This is not a game. The way we deal with data has a huge impact on how we make decisions. Taking time to logically think about what we need, how we get it, and what will we do with it can improve the data flow in the organization.

Simply stating "My boss asked for it" or "This is for the investors" is not enough. You must have a clear agenda before you ask someone to research the data. In the long term, you will learn to become more efficient by knowing exactly what you are after — and why — freeing others to do their work and freeing yourself from constantly extinguishing data fires that block creativity sparks.

Data Automation

Using data for easier decision-making means that data is available when we need to use it; most important, it will be available by the time we arrive in the office. For this reason, your data engineer must start the process during the night, having — at least — the most important parts of your data ready for you first thing in the morning. The most complicated calculations will not likely be needed until later in the day.

A key factor in the success of database automation is prioritizing; you need a clear priority for your views, and your data engineer must understand the way he must schedule processes, enabling you to consume the information *when you need it*.

Many managers have told me that all the data is important in the morning, but I learned to limit the amount of data I commit to in the morning run and, again, in the noon run. Using that approach, I've explained that they need to decide what is more important to know, i.e., the daily active users (DAUs) or how much money they spent on advertisement. Both processes are time-consuming, but we need to determine which is more important for business decision-making process. (Usually, the answer is cost; if we've overspent, we need to adjust the budget.)

Automating the runs requires strong consideration of the QA processes and failsafe mechanisms, making sure that wrong data won't be used by the teams in decision-making. The data engineer need not be in the office manually checking the data; it's enough to email

DATA AUTOMATION 87

during the process to indicate what is running, and this alerts people if something is not working as it should. For instance, a simple email saying the Facebook API didn't respond and we missed the data can save a great deal of time for the marketing department, reducing any feelings of mistrust at the same time.

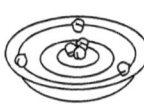

There's no question that consistency in hummus quality will create a long line outside the door. You don't need to have an expensive location or fine dining to bring people inside your place; you simply need to keep the quality of your hummus consistent day after day, have the right balance, and provide the balance to become a great hummus ambassador. Controlling quality ensures that people will return — and often bring friends with them!

Data QA is hugely important when it comes to building trust; too often, implementation of automatic reporting results in data consumers returning to Excel when/if the team loses trust in the data's integrity. To avoid this, our job is to ensure a good level of control over the data, setting flags in motion if things go in the wrong direction.

While it may sound like a lot of work, it's a simple process to raise a flag if something goes wrong. One starts by checking that all the data source's APIs are working and that the data extracts have arrived on the server. Next, check to make sure file sizes are similar to the historical data already in the system; if a size issue is found, we know we may have an issue with the data quality.

When downloading data, the number of columns may change often. I once used an API that needed to be rebuilt every other week because the data in it was always changing. Setting rules for what to do in such cases can be a time-saver. If the team says they have nothing to do with the report if the Facebook data is incomplete, or missing data columns, then the data engineer should mark it in his QA process as a reason to announce the process has failed. It doesn't mean the engineer did a bad job; it's just saving the data consumers from using data we know in advance won't be helpful. We should build the right process around it. If it's not important as having the revenue, then we can continue the processing of the data.

Maintaining a clear understanding of average numbers from previous days provides important information in regards to missing or corrupted data. This allows team members to quickly send emails, notifying data consumers that the data is significantly lower or higher, and that caution should be applied before using that data in decision-making.

Having this automatic information won't make your data more reliable, but it will make sure people don't need to QA the data daily (a job that can take two or three hours) just to reliably use your data. It's a pity we work so hard on structuring and automating the data — just to have people return to Excel because they don't trust the numbers coming from the data engineering team.

The main purpose of having reliable data available is to enable data consumers to make quick decisions and react to the market changes against the goals and targets they've been given. QA'ing the data helps them make easy decisions, knowing this is the best data they can get and that it was checked for issues. This also reduces stress levels when dealing with the optimization of millions — or deciding whether to keep or kill a new feature.

Many organizations I've worked with have a very open policy regarding SDKs on their app or trackers on their site, sharing a lot of information — worth a lot of money — with "partners" who used it for their own profit. Own your data; it's yours, you worked hard onboarding users, and there is no good reason to share this information with others, providing them free access to the assortment and the activity on your product.

By giving away your data to third-party sources, you are telling them what the user was searching for, how far he would go to convert,

DATA AUTOMATION

and whether he finalized the purchase. Consider an e-commerce site selling a variety of products; having a _unique_ product is very rare nowadays, and there will always be staunch competition in marketing that product. Telling Facebook that the user added the product to his basket — but never finalized the process — gives them all the information they need. In a month or two, they may try to convert your user at another site, selling your product (or something similar) to him because they now know how likely he is to convert, and what helps him pull the trigger on the sale.

The solution? Move away from the pull structure where we share data freely with third party partners. Instead, move into push data, where we share only what they need to know. If we wish to "muddy the waters," we mask and hash the data so they will not fully understand what we're doing. They are your partners — but also of your competition. Are you sure you wish to share all your information with them?

I had a long conversation with an organization pulling SDKs on their app, giving Facebook, Google, and others full access to their users. They weren't limited to the paid acquisition users, so when they were on your app or site, they had full access to organic users, CRM users, and other sources, allowing them to learn about the users and adapt the most efficient and effective advertising strategies. Even if you are a small company with few users, remember that data is GOLD; providing it at no cost to so-called "partners" may mean you lose important business.

It's critical to move into a push strategy where you provide only the information your partners need, uploading audiences, sending masked events, and withholding data from all users. Instead, provide only data relevant to your partner and business; after all, you never know where it is going or how it is being used, as no one provides a disclaimer as to how they will use it!

When I mention "push strategy," this refers to you obtaining the information, both _into_ your server and _from_ the server; you are firing the events into the competition. You can then randomize the money value or change a sensitive question into something no one will understand. It's vital to understand that today, with the GDPR law and the privacy laws in California, the game is different. Users want to know what is being done with their data, and while they want to trust us, it's not always clear that their info is safe. A lot of functions are trying to pull information from our organization (or from the user), and this information can be very sensitive. A breach of that information can kill our business.

Adapting a user-focused approach means we make the user an integral part of our design, accepting his decision as to what — and how — he shares with us. We have no business without users, so we must ensure that we provide him with a clear understanding of how we use his data, when we use it, when we delete it, and in what ways we share it with other partners.

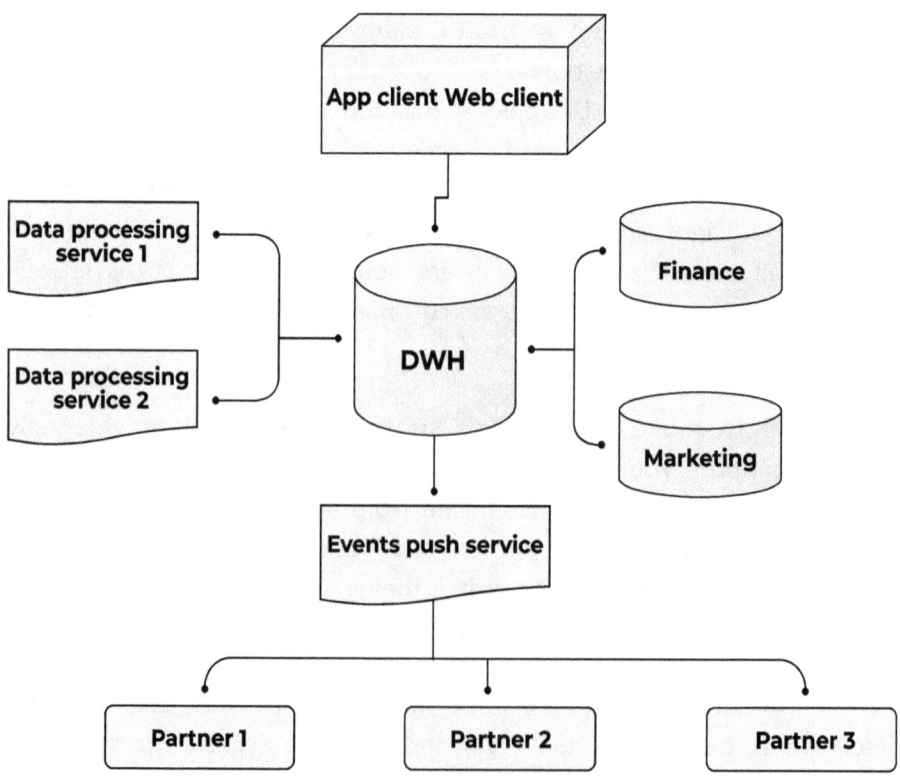

"Data-centric" means we are using the data, but most important, we must remain user-focused, with our data and product designers considering the privacy of the users, doing our best to control what information about him is shared with partners — and internally in the company. For instance, people in the marketing department need not have access to users' credit scores or credit cards. We must create layers of protection around our users to ensure we store their data and push it to our partners based on what we decide (and what the user allows.)

With this structure, we ensure that we transfer only the required data to the relevant sources — and only after we have anonymized it or aggregated it into a level of complication making it difficult to understand. However, we also create different sections for different partners, so we can distribute data across the organization and third parties without giving them the full access they wish to have.

Now, you have all the tools you need to become a data-centric team in the age of data noise, but let's dive deeper and discuss structure. As we depend more and more on data, we must adapt our teams to function in this new universe by driving more automation, by becoming more creative, and, above all, becoming more dynamic and focused on actions.

Team's Structure

To drive good results, we must change the way our organizations work, moving from old structures and manual processes towards more automation. Doing so requires a strong foundation of data and trust.

The roles of user acquisition (UA) and online marketing teams will change, shifting more and more away from manual work. The marketing department needs to focus on three approaches, each representing significant weight in terms of company success. The team must navigate data, driving impactable results from it. Some functions will need to be more "techy," others must be more creative, and the third approach involves a balance between the two, making sure they work optimally together, raising flags when they see that the ship is not moving fast enough.

The new data-driven team consists of three main positions:

- Supervisors — overseeing the spending and performance of the team, ensuring they work together flawlessly.
- Challengers — having soft skills and more focused on creativity. Based on his actions, data should become richer, more diverse, and providing the basis for deeper understanding.
- Controllers — working on building and maintaining the automatic machine, using the lessons of the challenger, and implementing them in the automation process.

All three functions — working as one unit — drive better performance for the entire organization.

Being any part of this team requires SQL knowledge, as members must dig into the data, researching and using it for optimizing their activity; no one should wait for someone else to help him extract the data he needs. SQL is simple to learn! It's not a programming language, and the logic required is as simple as that in a 4th-grade math class. Khan Academy — which I often recommend — has made it so easy to learn that an investment of two days will provide a basic understanding of it.

People with Python/R skills (or technical product management) will have a huge advantage, fitting well within the controller group. In past years, the libraries of these two languages have evolved into great, easy-to-use data structures and data analysis tools, allowing us to go over large amounts of data while driving stellar results from them. Such skills will greatly enhance any marketing automation tool you wish to build, from setting A/B testing to building predictive models in quick and simple ways.

When considering soft skills, we will need creative people who can think about concepts for personalization, understanding the users, and creating ads specifically tailored for them. Team members will need to be pragmatic and agile in implementing or testing new solutions to create fixed cycles of iterations. Data-centricity is not only about using the data, but also about using it in the *best way*, marrying the realms of *talking tech* and *thinking marketing*.

The controllers are the heart of the marketing department. These are people with great experience in marketing who adapted themselves into the technology world; they can lead the automation project, speaking comfortably with developers. These team members take the challengers' outcomes, translating the research into lessons, maintaining the automation tool using the best knowledge and data available. Thanks to them, each euro invested drives optimal results based on the knowledge available.

The controllers' profile includes marketing experience mixed with some programming experience, so they understand the challenges and issues the developers may have in the implementation process.

They also possess product management training to assist them in prioritizing and raising issues in the right way.

The challengers represent the "chaos" of the marketing department — in a good way! Their job is to think about new ways to engage with the users, testing them, creating a proof-of-concept, and helping the company machine improve. They sit with data scientists, coming up with new things to test, from changing the Call to Action (CTA) to verifying new partners, designing a test frame. Once their concept is proven, it moves to the controllers who implement it within the machine. They need to work "guerrilla-style," maximizing each euro they must prove that the system can do better. Their profile: marketing experts with SQL to extract and research the data, along with statistical experience, enabling them to test things in the right way.

The supervisors are on the management level, and their job is to investigate research and raise issues regarding the function of both teams; the controllers who focus on maintaining the product and the challengers who find new ways to improve the business. Supervisors balance allocating the budget and *questioning the use of it*. They must have great accounting skills, and the ability to use SQL to get the data they need. The rules they set help the controllers and challengers focus on creating lasting impacts on the company's bottom line.

In the future, marketing demands the use of SQL and the need for skilled technical members dedicated to becoming data-centric, driving more personalization, and better insights from the users. They will work together like a finely tuned speed boat, reacting purposefully and quickly to changes, dedicated to improving the user experience, and meeting all company goals in a fluid environment.

Data engineers and developers should define the work and set the priorities, instead of accepting delays created by engineers whose focus is geared solely on a single business function.

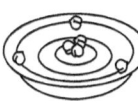

Hummus is first mentioned in the Bible. Not many know this, but the dish was based on chickpeas, left in water to become fermented. Farmers used to eat it in the morning, with the belief that it was a power food, enabling them to stay full for the workday. Later, someone thought of cooking the chickpeas and then mixing them in tahini. This dish was already improved by someone with a bit more creativity and with the understanding that taste is important.

Summing up

We've talked about what we need to do to become data-centric and considered the risks for industries in terms of new laws and regulations aimed at reducing adverse breaches of user data. There are ways to work around these challenges, but teams will need to be focused on data strategy, discovering workarounds to laws by anonymizing the data, aggregating it in a statistical way that allows us to keep using it.

Using the Data Discovery Workshop, you can find a clear path to decision-making by simplifying your databases and avoiding issues with authorities in terms of data collection and disbursement. The workshop documentation will help you explain the rationale for your decisions and allow you to communicate more efficiently — and honestly — with your users.

Having data requests, analysis documentation, and using tickets to track them all will assist in following salient regulations. Develop and use tickets, organizing them so it tracks all activity, allowing other team members to easily understand and follow each step taken. As a very wise monk once said, "You may be the first one to sit on the toilet, but you are not the last. Keep it clean and organized, don't let your mind carry you away from the task of now".

We need to stop using Excel — or any other method requiring excessive energy to consume our data. We shouldn't be doing manual calculations, as this provides the greatest avenue for errors. Automation creates more efficiency, but keep your eyes peeled for changes and challenges, so you aren't wasting days on mindless analysis via the usage of Excel.

In fast-moving industries, we must be both dynamic and fast. The only way to do that effectively is by having a clear strategy that reduces the amount of data we consume daily, and reducing any inefficient analyses we run, the kind of analysis that leaves us with more questions and less understanding of how to use the data provided.

Data can be our most valuable tool, but only when gathered and used properly with clear goals and expectations. Combining different events and data sources into a user score (or session score) allows us to decide what matters most: user conversion, or user retention. Unless we build the data strategy according to company goals and expectations, learning what works and what doesn't, we will drown in a sea (or data lake) of useless statistics that do little to pay bills and garner more business.

Laws such as GDPR, ePrivacy in Europe, and privacy regulations in California will raise challenges for product and marketing departments, limiting their access to user data. This will cause increased ghost users, requiring more out-of-the-box thinking to convince users to opt-in for tracking in order to provide us with useful data in our organizations.

Experience in SQL and Python may become a must-have for anyone wishing to work with data; understanding the importance of asking "Why?" and reducing complex problems into simple actions will become leading skills for any business. As we become more structured in our thinking to create long- and short-term strategies, teams will replace copy/paste and "put-out-the-fire" mentalities with better approaches to understanding important data.

I hope this book helps you and your team garner better results as you improve the way you think about data, how you gather it, and, most important, how and why you need to reduce data noise in your organization.

Cook more data!

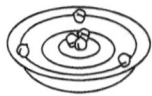

When a hummus dish is served, most of us don't see the process those chickpeas went through! We see a dish sitting before us, judging its looks first, and then taste it to decide whether we like it or not. Our reports are very similar to a hummus plate: we don't know the process the data went through. We might guess what took place, we might look and digest the data, but find ourselves hungry for more just a short while later.

In hummus, we use dry chickpeas, soaking them in water before cooking, and cleaning to remove any stones so no one breaks a tooth. Likewise, data must be processed in a way that makes it useful — and safe — for your organization.

The recipe used for your hummus was likely prepared hundred- if not thousands — of times before. It was "QA'ed" for errors and improved many times to arrive at the product the owner is proud enough to serve. He learned a lot about preparation of his special dish, researching ingredients, finding the best chickpeas, the perfect tahini and olive oil, and he mixed them until he created an experience you'll return to repeatedly.

Learning your data and understanding what works within your strategy will make you proud of your "dish." You'll be happy to share it around, but above all, it will help you stay consistent on your decisions, understanding them better and driving more value for your clients.

Understanding the right balance of ingredients in your "dish" is also critical to your outcome. Adding chickpeas on top — like a garnish — is nice, but the difference between adding 10 or 25 doesn't have much effect on the hummus itself. That said, having the right amount of tahini WILL make a difference; too much or too little will keep the customers away!

SUMMING UP

Understanding your clients leads to repeat business and good reviews. In the restaurant business, one way of checking satisfaction involves looking at the leftovers. If a lot of hummus is left on the dish, you may have problems. In data, you must check to see if your user followed the funnel as you intended.

In the end, hummus is a very simple dish, using chickpeas, water, olive oil, garlic, and tahini. Keeping it simple is critical in terms of consistency and return customers, and there's no need to add truffles or avocado, which only serve to crate expensive and complex experiences for customers.

Usually, the best hummus locations are not in fancy places; often, they are in shady or suspect areas where you wonder if you'll survive the experience! This, too, points to simplicity. The same concept applies to your reports: keep them simple. These aren't paintings, they are reports, designed to help people make good decisions.

I hope this book didn't inspire you to open a hummus restaurant; that's *my* exit plan! Seriously, I hope you garnered a more direct path in terms of using your data to drive better decisions and learned the importance of protecting that data.

If you wish to download my workshop's canvas files (empty for your use) feel free to visit www.hummus-club.com

Thank you for reading!

Before you go, I'd love to share my recipe for hummus:

Ingredients

500 g dry chickpeas

1 carrot

1 small onion

2 teaspoons baking powder

5-7 cloves of garlic

25 g parsley, roughly chopped

Tahini

¼ teaspoon of cumin

Juice from one lemon

Preparation

- Rinse the chickpeas, place them in a large bowl covered with cold water, and leave to soak for 12 hours. They will double in size, so make sure the bowl is large enough to hold them.

- Strain the water, wash the chickpeas and cover them with water for another 12 hours. Add half of the baking powder — this is the trick to achieving a smooth and creamy consistency.

- 12 hours later, add the chickpeas to a large pot. Combine with the onion, carrot, and 1 clove of garlic. Simmer for an hour.

- Add the rest of the baking powder, and let the chickpeas cook until you can easily mash them between your fingers.

- Take ⅔ of the chickpeas, cooling them under ice water, pulling the shells from as many as you can.

- Place the chickpeas in a blender with the rest of the garlic, add the cooking water as needed to achieve a velvety texture.

- With the blender still running, add cumin, parsley, tahini (the secret is to have ⅓ tahini and ⅔ chickpeas) and lemon juice, adjusting the quantities to your taste.

www.ingramcontent.com/pod-product-compliance
Lightning Source LLC
Chambersburg PA
CBHW050244220526
45465CB00002B/544